BLACK MAGISTRATES

A Study of Selection and Appointment

by

MICHAEL KING
and COLIN MAY

The Cobden Trust
1985

The Cobden Trust
21 Tabard Street
London SE1 4LA

The Trust's publications do not necessarily reflect the views of the Trust.

British Library Cataloguing in Publication Data

King, Michael, *1942-*
    Black magistrates: selection and appointment.
    1. Police magistrates — England.   2. Blacks — England
    I. Title   II. May, Colin
    344.207'16   KD7309

ISBN 0-900137-24-X

Printed in Great Britain
by the Russell Press, Nottingham

BLACK MAGISTRATES

FOREWORD

Ninety per cent of criminal cases are dealt with in magistrates' courts, the vast majority by lay magistrates. It is therefore essential that the magistracy should be representative of the community. This involves appointment of magistrates from all social classes and all social groups.

Magistrates are appointed by the Lord Chancellor on the recommendation of Advisory Committees, which usually have Sub-Committees which function as selection committees. The Advisory Committees and the Selection Committees should also be representative of the whole community.

Black Magistrates analyses the problems surrounding the provision of black magistrates. It examines the system of appointment of magistrates and highlights the importance of the Advisory Committees as selection committees, pinpointing their weaknesses.

The authors suggest improved methods of selection, aimed at extending the field of selection, refining the way in which it is carried out, and clarifying its objectives.

They also recommend extension and improvement of the training programme and that it should precede recommendation to the Lord Chancellor for appointment. This report is worthy of careful study.

Pitt of Hampstead

ACKNOWLEDGEMENTS

First and foremost our thanks must go to Sarah Spencer, The Cobden Trust's Director, not only for her organisational and administrative skills, but also for her patience and enthusiasm throughout all stages of this report's preparation. It is hard for us to imagine how this report could have been published without her help and advice.

We are grateful for the financial support we received from the Commission for Racial Equality and from those who provided funding for The Cobden Trust. We hope that this report justifies their investment. Thank you also to the administrative staff of Warwick University Law School, and particularly to Helen Beresford and Sally Venables.

Most of our research would have been impossible without the co-operation of members of the Lord Chancellor's Department and Duchy of Lancaster's Office. They not only answered our many questions with courtesy and patience, but they also encouraged Advisory Committees to complete our postal questionnaires. The National Council of Community Relations Councils also gave its support in agreeing to distribute our questionnaires.

Our thanks to Sara Kearney and Paul Gordon for their help in preparing the report and to Lisa Freedman for her copy editing.

Our particular thanks must go to all those busy people, including representatives of black community organisations, Community Relations Councils, Advisory Committees and the many magistrates, who were willing to give their time to be interviewed during our local studies.

Finally, our gratitude to those who read through and gave us their invaluable comments on the drafts of this report. They are Joyce Redfearn, Vinod Kumar, Malcolm Hurwitt, Christine Jackson and Peter Wallington

Michael King
Colin May

CONTENTS

Part 1:

THE ISSUES:
CIVIL LIBERTIES, JUSTICE AND THE MAGISTRACY

Chapter 1

CIVIL LIBERTIES AND BLACK MAGISTRATES

The appointment of black* magistrates raises several important questions concerning the nature of contemporary British society. There is the obvious issue of racial prejudice. Does it exist even in institutions such as the magistracy which lie at the heart of the British establishment institutions which should be setting an example to others through the fairness and impartiality with which they conduct their affairs? Secondly, there is the issue of community justice. Is the magistracy representative of the local community? Does it represent the interests of the local community on the Bench?† Does the community see it that way? Do all law-abiding groups within the community see the magistracy as representing their interests? More specifically, it raises questions about the way in which magistrates are chosen. Is the system of selection efficient? Is it just? Does it meet the criteria of openness and fairness that one should expect from a system responsible for appointing people to judicial office? Finally, there is the issue of the role of the lay magistracy within the criminal and civil justice systems. Is the use of unpaid members of the judiciary really workable in an economically depressed society where jobs are at a premium and most people either cannot afford, or cannot risk, taking time off work to do their public duty on the magistrates' Bench?

All of these questions are relevant to our research. They situate the subject of our enquiry at the crossroads of two major contemporary preoccupations: race relations and the administration of justice. Yet much of the contemporary debate over race relations and the administration of justice is conducted in

---

*We use the term 'black' throughout this report to refer to people of African, West Indian or Asian origin who emigrated to this country or were born here.

† We use the term 'Bench' with a capital 'B' to denote all the magistrates with a particular Petty Sessional Division or Commission and with a small 'b' to refer to the magistrates sitting in one courtroom.

an haphazard and ill-informed way, usually in response to some 'sensational' event such as the court cases following the street disturbances of 1981, or the trials of groups of black people arising out of confrontations with the police.

Little systematic research has been conducted. Little is actually known about black people in relation to the courts. Impressionistic accounts and limited empirical evidence suggest that they are more likely to be prosecuted than white people, and that a disproportionate number of black people appear to end up in prison, youth custody centres and detention centres.[1] Why this should be so is still a matter of speculation or, alternatively, for accusations of deliberate racial discrimination on the part of police, magistrates and judges.

Similarly, despite several well-intentioned media attempts to peer behind the formal edifice of justice,[2] the machinery which appoints Justices of the Peace remains, for most people, a mystery. Even if they are aware of the existence of the Lord Chancellor's Advisory Committees (A.C.s), very few know how these committees work, the sort of people who sit on them, or the criteria they apply in making their decisions.

We saw our initial role, therefore, as one of demystification. In terms of magistrates decisions, we sought to clarify the processes whereby differences in cultural and racial background and experiences stemming from these differences might influence decision-making (Chapter 2). We also set out to clarify the mechanism for the selection and appointment of magistrates, not only at the formal level, but also in relation to the complex relationship between the Lord Chancellor and his Department, local magistrates and local political parties (Chapter 4).

For our empirical research, we decided that it was not sufficient merely to present a statistical account. We realised that it was important to obtain sufficient statistical information to present a general picture of the number of black magistrates in different areas and to provide some indication of the types of black people who were being appointed to the Bench. But we also wanted to identify those factors, be they party political, philosophical, economic or cultural, which influenced the decisions both of the candidates in putting their names forward and of the selectors in rejecting them or recommending them for appointment. However, we accepted that our main job was to concentrate upon the process of selection itself and not, for example, upon the complexities of the local political scene and the extent of black people's involvement in local politics.

Faced with the realisation that the subject of our research could not be isolated from everything else that was going on in the social world and, wishing at the same time not to stray too far from the narrow confines of the selection and appointments system, we decided to make every effort to relate our investigations of individual behaviour, the explanations given by people for their own behaviour and their perceptions of the behaviour of others to factors outside the confines of the appointment system as formally or officially defined. It is through this approach that we attempt to identify the social forces which influence the individual's behaviour and attitudes. Decisions about people are, therefore, seen, not so much as the application of abstract principles to particular cases, but as the product of institutional structures, role demands and the decision-makers' perception of the people concerned, based upon his or her values, beliefs and experiences and upon exchanges with other decision makers. A full account of our research method is set out at the start of Chapter 3.

As far as possible we tried to let people speak for themselves about those issues which we had identified as being important for our research. This does not mean that we claim complete objectivity for our study. Necessarily we embarked upon this project with pre-existing values and beliefs and no doubt these influenced the manner in which we conducted our research and our interpretation of the results.

Moreover, we make no secret of the fact that some of the things we discovered about the present system and some of the attitudes of those responsible for its operation conflicted with our own viewpoint. However, we have in the account of our research results deliberately tried to avoid drawing attention to our own, often critical views, since what we are trying to present in our account of the appointment system's operation in relation to black people is a serious piece of research which captures as fully and as accurately as possible its subtleties and complexities, and is not merely a piece of polemic.

How then does this relate to civil liberties? In the first place, our preconceptions, when translated into a research strategy, determined the sorts of issues we wanted to examine and the sorts of questions we wanted to ask the people whom we interviewed. These preconceptions were based upon the ideal principles of openness and accountability in the selection of people for public office and of the need of a liberal society to protect its minorities against discrimination and injustice. These principles gave rise at the start of our research to a number of specific statements concerning the minimum requirements that any society which respected civil liberties would wish to be present in its system for selecting lay magistrates. These were:

1. The make-up of the body of magistrates operating in any

5

court should reflect the local population served by the court. This means that all sectors of the local community should be represented on the Bench roughly in accordance with their numbers in the local population. The sort of factors to be taken into account in establishing a representative Bench should include not only social class, age, race and gender, but also attitudes towards the sort of issues that are likely to come before the court. Ideally the magistrates should therefore reflect a cross-section of attitudes towards the police and sentencing.

2.   The system for selecting magistrates should be fair to all candidates. It should not in any way discriminate either directly or indirectly against some sectors of the community or give an advantage to others, except insofar as discrimination in selection is necessary to ensure that magistrates are able to perform the tasks required of them on the Bench.

3.   Where candidates are rejected, it should be because of their failure to meet clearly established criteria relating specifically to tasks which magistrates are required to perform on the Bench.

4.   The conditions of service of magistrates should not be such as to exclude certain sectors of the community or discourage them from applying to join the Bench.

5.   The system of selection should be open to public scrutiny. the only justification for secrecy is the protection of the interests of candidates.

6.   There should be effective safeguards against the Bench in any area being dominated by one or more interest groups and against 'self-perpetuation' resulting from control over the appointments system by local magistrates.

7.   Every effort should be made to ensure that both the magistracy and the way magistrates are selected enjoy the support of the local community, including minority groups within that community.

Although we decided against confining our research to a simple examination of the present system in the light of these statements, as this would have meant ignoring much that was important and interesting in the broader issue of black people and the magistracy, we did decide that it would be essential, if our report were to tackle the civil-liberty questions raised by the selection process, to return to these statements after we had set out our findings. The final chapter of our report, therefore, uses these statements as a yardstick against which to assess the selection system; and they serve as a basis for our discussion on how the system might be improved and for our specific proposals for change.

Chapter 2

BLACK MAGISTRATES AND JUSTICE

Calls for more black people to be in positions of power and responsibility have multiplied since the street violence of 1981. So much so that it is now difficult to find any one in government or the senior civil service who does not at least pay lip-service to policies which encourage black people to participate in the management of the country's social institutions. This was certainly true of those officials responsible for the selection and appointment of magistrates with whom we spoke at the start of our research. Yet the longer our research went on the clearer it became that the reasoning behind the 'official' view that there should be more black magistrates was different from the motives which inspired us to carry out this project.

Within the Lord Chancellor's Department and among the Lord Chancellor's Advisory Committees there appeared to be a genuine concern that the magistrates' Bench in any area should be representative of the local community, including any ethnic minorities within that community. An unrepresentative Bench, so the reasoning went, is unlikely to gain the confidence of those sections of society who are unrepresented or under-represented and the justice dispensed by the magistrates' court is therefore unlikely to be acceptable to them. What was lacking was any suggestion that the background and cultural characteristics of J.P.s, including racial background and characteristics, might affect the nature and quality of the justice they dispense. Indeed, behind the apparent support for black magistrates there seemed to be a complacent and simplistic notion of how justice is done and who is competent to dispense it.

Magistrates' decision-making tended to be seen in objective, absolute terms. There is one right decision, one proper sentence, one valid conclusion to be drawn from the evidence. Thus the secretary of one Advisory Committee told us that the purpose of the selection interview was to 'find out what is this person, what is the quality of this person, will they be able to solve the evidence, to sort out the evidence and make a decision in discussion with people.'

7

Judicial decision-making in magistrates' courts was presented to us as the drawing of logical inferences from the evidence and we were told that the sort of people capable of such justice were 'well-balanced' men and women with 'commonsense', 'unbiased' and without 'extreme attitudes'. Absent from this official view was any notion that values and beliefs might have their part to play in magistrates' justice. 'I cannot understand what having a knowledge of the background and attitudes of ethnic minority groups has got to do with law enforcement.' (former member Lord Chancellor's Advisory Committee).

It was not only officialdom which presented us with this simple, depersonalised view of justice. Very similar ideas were expressed to us by a small number of the representatives of Afro-Caribbean and Asian communities whom we interviewed, who were by and large very critical of magistrates' courts. They saw the magistracy as a faceless, impersonal body of bureaucrats whose function was to enforce the law by convicting and punishing those that the police brought before them. According to this view, it made not the slightest difference whether magistrates were white or black, or whether they came from middle-class or working-class backgrounds, since, on joining the Bench, they would adopt its existing values and suppress their own beliefs and perceptions in order to perform their judicial functions according to the law. In their view individual J.P.s had virtually no freedom of action, so that the appointment of more black magistrates was a non-issue.

Thus, the officials responsible for the functioning of the appointments system and some of the fiercest critics of the magistracy agreed that, so far as the quality of justice was concerned, the colour of individual magistrates was of scant importance. It is a conclusion with which we profoundly disagree and, since this issue is so central to our research, we have devoted this second chapter to a presentation of the evidence, both direct and indirect, which suggests that the characteristics of individual decision-makers may indeed play an important part in judicial decision-making.

So, what do we know about decisions in judicial settings? The statistics from official sources and research studies indicate quite clearly that whenever magistrates exercise discretionary powers, for example, in sentencing, bail and legal-aid decisions, considerable variations exist from court to court. These variations are not, moreover, attributable simply to different police practices or local conditions in various parts of the country.[3] One study found, for example, that the use of prison as a punishment varied between 3 per cent of adult male offenders at one magistrates' court and 19 per cent at another.[4] Tarling, the author of this study suggested that 'court traditions' rather than individual differences among magistrates played an important part in determining the policies of Benches and it was these different policies which were the major obstacle to achieving greater consistency between courts (p.45). However, Roger Hood, in an important study of the sentencing of motoring offenders (1972), concluded that, 'there is a good deal of evidence that personal characteristics, attitudes and experience affect both the items of information which are chosen and the way that information is interpreted and used' (p.10).

A recent study of decisions by Mental Health Tribunal members[5] took matters a little further by showing that where the evidence was finely balanced in a simulated tribunal hearing, the decision-makers tended to draw upon their backgrounds and professional training in determining whether the patient should be released or kept in hospital. Thus, psychiatrists were much more likely than lawyers to opt for continued hospitalisation, although both professional groups had been presented with exactly the same evidence.

Both these studies, it must be emphasised, were concerned with individual decision-making, whereas lay magistrates, of course, usually sit as a bench of three or more justices. Moreover, Hood's study took the form of a written sentencing exercise sent to the magistrates' homes which may have reduced the effect of court traditions and policies in sentencing which Tarling considered to be so important. However, firm evidence that the characteristics of individual justices may affect decisions even in the context of the magistrates' Bench in real-life cases now exists.

David Farrington and Allison Morris (1983 [i] and [ii]) recently published the results of research they had carried out on differences between sentencing by men and women magistrates. These showed that where male magistrates were in the majority on the bench less than 10 per cent of women offenders received a severe sentence compared to 19 per cent in those courts where women magistrates were in the majority on the bench hearing the case. Quite independently of court policies, therefore, individual differences among magistrates may influence the sorts of decisions they make.

None of this research, however, throws any light on the psychological processes which may account for these differences in decision-making, whether they be between different courts or individual magistrates. Yet Bond and Lemon (1978), in their study of magistrates' training, have been able to show a socialisation process at work in respect of some new recruits to the Bench. The attitudes of many of these recruits on issues relevant to court decisions appeared to change significantly during their period of training, gradually falling in line with the attitudes of existing members of the Bench. According to Elizabeth Burney (1979), however, the ease with which benches of magistrates appear to reach consensus in their decision-making is a reflection of the selection process rather than any training programme. The selectors, she claims, tend to choose a 'clubbable' type of person (p.115). This sort of person will, she adds, 'fit in with the team' and will defer to the knowledge and experience of their senior colleagues on the bench, particularly the chairperson (p.113). Yet, it would be foolish to suggest that every magistrate is equally conformist. In Bond and Lemon's study, for example, there was considerable variation among new magistrates in the extent to which they assimilated the attitudes of existing J.P.s.

Moreover, the recent study of differences between men and women magistrates' sentencing decisions would suggest that the process is much more complex than straightforward socialisation or assimiliation. Most Benches do have implicit tariffs for certain common offences and also certain unwritten policies on bail and legal aid[6] and all justices at that court are expected to conform to these policies in their decision-making. However, many cases that come before the courts are not amenable to simple rule-of-thumb decisions, but raise issues which require decision-makers to draw upon their individual attitudes and beliefs. It is here that the different characteristics of magistrates, including racial and cultural backgrounds, may be important.

Julie Vennard (1982) of the Home Office Research and Planning Unit recently identified one major category of cases where these factors are likely to play a major part in the bench's decision. She carried out a detailed study of magistrates' decisions in contested cases, analysing 373 such cases in order to try and establish some relationship between the evidence presented to the court and the final result of 'guilty' or 'not guilty'. As might be expected, there was a strong correlation between attempts to 'impugn the credibility' of the defendant and/or the defence witnesses and subsequent convictions by the court. These attempts took the form of the prosecution pointing out inconsistencies in the defendant's explanation — casting doubt on the 'general credit' of the defendant by, for example, showing that the defendant was drunk at the time and had no clear recollection of events; or by emphasising the 'inherent improbability' in the defendant's story — the handler of stolen goods, for example, who claims they were sold to him by an unknown person in a pub. What was particularly interesting about Vennard's analysis, however, was her finding that even where the defendant's credibility had not been challenged or impugned, 63 per cent of charges still resulted in conviction. Moreover in only 3 per cent of those cases had the defendant previously confessed to the offence. In the main the prosecution case rested entirely on police eyewitness accounts of the defendant's conduct and the criminal intent tacit in his/her behaviour (p.21).

Vennard, in her conclusions, states that her findings 'confirm the tendency for magistrates to accept prosecution eyewitness evidence of the defendant's behaviour as against a denial of the alleged conduct or a contention that the act did not constitute a crime' (p.21). Vennard goes on to suggest that magistrates may not be sufficiently familiar with the results of research into eyewitness accuracy, even where the eyewitnesses are police officers. Yet this suggestion misses the point that even if magistrates were knowledgeable on this subject, their knowledge alone would not, in the vast majority of cases, help them to decide whose version of events was the more accurate, that of the police or the defendant. Moreover, if lack of knowledge of psychological evidence on potential police eyewitness inaccuracy is to be a sufficient explanation for Vennard's results, she would have to explain why juries, who might be expected to have even less knowledge than magistrates on this subject, nevertheless appear to be more sceptical of police evidence, acquitting in a higher proportion of contested cases. A far more likely explanation is that of a 'perceptual set' among many magistrates which predisposes them to accept the evidence of the police unless there are very strong grounds indeed for doubting the police officer's word. Indeed, Burney, from her interviews with magistrates, was able to produce some evidence for just such a perceptual set (pp.184-188).

However, we don't intend to discuss yet again whether or not magistrates are more police orientated than juries in their decisions. Our purpose in quoting these studies is rather to show that the characteristics of individual magistrates may indeed influence decision-making and that the potential for such influence is strongest in those cases where the evidence before the court does not point strongly in one direction or another. It occurs, in other words, where decisions cannot be made purely on the basis of logical inference, where there is uncertainty as to what happened or what is likely to happen in the future.[7] This uncertainty may be particularly marked in those cases where the Bench is required to make decisions which relate to an attempt to predict a person's future conduct, as in bail decisions, sentencing and care cases. In cases involving uncertainty the question which magistrates frequently have to answer, often on the basis of flimsy evidence, is 'What sort of person are we dealing with?' Just how people cope with this question has for some time occupied the minds of social psychologists who define the issue as one of 'person perception'.

In their textbook on social psychology Secord & Backman (1964) write:

> Often an opinion concerning the other person is not based on direct observation of him but on statements by others or on knowledge of who he is. Moreover, *opinions, evaluations* or *feelings* involve *subjective judgement and inference* that go beyond the kind of direct sensory impressions that characterise perception (p.49). (Our emphasis)

There is also considerable evidence from studies carried out by psychologists that in the absence of definite knowledge, these subjective *'opinions, evaluations or feelings'* are used by people, firstly to 'fill in' gaps in the information they have about others (see Asch, 1946) and, secondly, to make judgements, both ascriptive and predictive about other people's behaviour. Theories of person perception, such as attribution theory and personal construct theory, are based upon a wealth of experimental results demonstrating how people make use of their preconceptions in their judgement of the behaviour of others and in their predictions as to their future behaviour. Since the Harrisburg Seven trial in America in 1977 psychologists have even been used by lawyers to assist them in the selection of jurors.[8] The most celebrated example of this was the Angela Davies trial where detailed portraits of potential jurors were accumulated and assessed by teams of psychologists in an attempt to ensure that those who might be predisposed to convict were not selected for the jury.

However, while it is clear that attitudes and background do affect legal decision-making, the relationship is by no means as straightforward as some commentators would have us believe. There is no evidence, for example, to support the view that people from particular ethnic groups or socio-economic classes will tend to favour those from the same group or class in their decisions. Indeed, evidence from a previous study would seem to suggest that where magistrates' sentencing decisions are concerned the opposite may be the case, working-class magistrates being more severe than their middle-class colleagues (Pearson, 1981, p.81). But the same study found that working-class magistrates 'shared considerable scepticism towards police behaviour and the evidence they gave in court' (pp.81-2). Moreover, the Farrington and Morris (1983) study mentioned earlier clearly indicates that women magistrates are tougher than men on some female offenders. The most that can be said is that magistrates, like everyone else, differ in their perceptions of people, the interpretations they place on their conduct and the predictions they make about their future behaviour. Such differences are likely to be most marked in cases involving inadequate information or uncertainty which make it difficult or impossible to reach decisions by logical inference or the simple application of a formula. These differences in perception, interpretation and prediction are in part, at least, a product of experience, education, cultural and social background. Of course one does not want to appoint as magistrates people who are overtly prejudicial or incapable of deductive reasoning. On the other hand, it is surely wrong not to recognise among potentially suitable candidates the part played by culture, background and experiences in decision-making and to avoid any consideration of these differences in selecting the magistracy.

Part 2:

THE SELECTION AND APPOINTMENTS SYSTEM

Chapter 3

METHODS OF RESEARCH

The general aim of our research was to find out as much as possible about the recruitment of black people to the magistrates', Bench. We were interested not only in the formal system of selection and rejection, but also in the structure of power and influence underlying the process and in the beliefs, attitudes and experiences of those involved in the system as administrators, selectors and successful and unsuccessful candidates.

Yet, in order to find out how the system works in relation to black candidates, it is necessary not only to investigate the selection process, but also to examine how black people come to be candidates in the first place. Thus, we considered it an important part of our research to ascertain the extent to which black people put their names forward and the factors involved in their decision to become candidates and whether applications from black people arose through their involvement in particular sorts of organisations. We were more interested in discovering what contacts, if any, existed between black people and black organisations on the one hand and local Advisory Committees and Sub-Committees (S.C.s) on the other. We wanted to know about the attitudes to and experiences of the selection process of officers and executive members of Afro-Caribbean and Asian organisations and community relations groups, who might themselves have been approached to become candidates for the Bench, or who might, either as individuals or as representatives of their organisations, have encouraged (or discouraged) others to apply for selection.

Furthermore, we believed it was essential for us to discover how many black magistrates there were, particularly in areas where the black population was high. We wanted to know whether the numbers of black J.P.s reflected the local black population both numerically and in terms of class background and attitudes. We found out early in our research that no information of this sort existed.[9] Indeed, the Lord Chancellor's Department was unable to tell us even the overall number of black magistrates in the country. The absence of any information, either official or unofficial made this aspect of our research even more important.

All the data collection and field work for the research was carried out during the first eight months of 1983. Given our very broad brief, we decided on what may be termed 'a blanket approach'. This consisted, first, of undertaking two postal surveys. In the first postal survey a questionnaire was distributed to a sample of forty-four local Advisory Committees and the Clerks to the Justices of the eighty-three Petty Sessional Divisions which fell within their areas of responsibility. These questionnaires were accompanied by a letter from the Deputy Secretary of Commissions of the Lord Chancellor's Department stating that the Lord Chancellor had 'no objection to this research' and expressing the hope that the recipients 'would find it possible to assist the researcher'. Both the questionnaires and the letter are reproduced in Appendices One and Two. Included in the sample were all the areas in England and Wales where, according to the 1981 Census, Afro-Caribbeans and Asians combined were 4.5 per cent or more of the local population. We received replies from thirty-five Advisory Committees (79.5 per cent) and from fifty-seven Petty Sessional Divisions within the areas covered by these Advisory Committees. We also received completed questionnaires from an additional four Petty Sessional Divisions, making a total of sixty-one (73.5 per cent). In addition, seven of the most interesting responses from A.C.s were followed by telephone interviews with the secretary.

The other postal survey consisted of a questionnaire sent to all Community Relations Councils and equivalent organisations in England and Wales as at April 1982, listed in the Commission for Racial Equality's List of Community Relations Councils 1983. From the 101 sent out, we received fifty-nine replies, a response rate of 58.4 per cent. This questionnaire is also reproduced in Appendix Two.

Through these two sets of questionnaires we were able to obtain useful information about such matters as the numbers and occupational background of existing black magistrates and the number of years they had been sitting on the Bench. We were also able to discover what contacts existed between local Advisory Committees and Community Relations Councils and Afro-Caribbean and Asian organisations and what attempts had been made to increase such contacts. The Community Relations Council questionnaire replies told us, moreover, something about the attitudes of the members of these organisations and of the local black population towards the recruitment process and towards the magistrates who dispensed justice in their area. Much of this information is set out in Chapters 12 and 13.

We should mention at this stage a problem which we encountered in our attempt to obtain accurate statistics for the Afro-Caribbean and Asian populations to be used, for example, in our comparisons of the magistrates' Bench with the proportion of black people in the local population. Although the 1981 Census did not contain an 'ethnic-group question' and, therefore, does not provide any direct information on the numbers of Afro-Caribbean or Asians living in any one area, it is nonetheless useful as the most comprehensive and up-to-date source of population figures, providing data on the geographical origins of all heads of households. Thus, for the purpose of our research, we were able to estimate approximately the black populations of specific areas by assuming that it could be represented by all those people 'usually resident' in households of which the head was born in the Caribbean, India, East Africa, Bangladesh or Pakistan. This assumption, of course, has the effect of including white people born in these areas, but excluding Afro-Caribbeans and Asians born in this country who have set up their own households. It is generally agreed among population analysts that this assumption is likely to give an underestimate of the actual black population.[10] For the areas covered in our local studies, described below, we were able to supplement the 'district level' census figures with 'small area statistics' in order to obtain estimates of the local black population.

The second element of our research strategy was to go and visit five pre-selected areas and interview secretaries, chairpersons and members of Advisory and Sub-Committees, magistrates, unsuccessful black candidates for the magistracy, Asian and Afro-Caribbean community representatives, and office holders and members of Community Relations Councils.

Our choice of areas was based upon our wish to include in our local study as broad a range of different black communities as possible. In two of the areas studied, therefore, Branston and Meadowport*, black people make up between 4 and 6 per cent of the local population and are roughly equally divided between Afro-Caribbeans and Asians (mainly Indians). The black communities in these two areas were established in the 1950s. In Thorburn, on the other hand, the black community has represented a significant part of the local population since well before the migrations of the 1950s and is probably one of the oldest established black communities in the country. Metropole County was chosen because it covered a large suburban area with a combined Afro-Caribbean and Asian (again mainly Indian) community estimated to be almost 15 per

*All the place names used in this report are fictitious in order to maintain the confidentiality promised to interviewees.

19

cent of the local population. We concentrated our research on three Petty Sessional Divisions within this area. Harley, the last of our five local study areas also has a black community which constitutes about 15 per cent of the local population, but here the black people concerned are almost entirely of Pakistani origin and it was for this reason that we included the area in our study. A description of all five of these areas is given in Appendix IV.

All the interviews we undertook were semi-structured, that is to say that the interviewer was armed with a list of open-ended questions which he put to the interviewees as unobtrusively as possible in an attempt to direct the conversation to those particular areas which concerned us. A list of the questions we used is set out in Appendix III. Our interviewer for all the interviews was white, in his early thirties and with no discernible accent. All the interviews were conducted one-to-one with four exceptions. On two occasions two people were interviewed jointly and in two other instances three and four people were interviewed together. We interviewed people in a wide variety of locations ranging from court offices to pubs, cafés and living-rooms. Whenever the interviewees agreed, the interview was recorded on tape and the tapes subsequently listened to by the interviewer and independently by one other member of the research team. If consent to record was not given, notes were made during the interview and these were 'written out' by the interviewer at the first opportunity after the interview. In addition to people within the five local study areas we also interviewed the chairman of another Advisory Committee and conducted short telephone interviews with the secretaries of seven other Advisory Committees A.C.s or Sub-Committees S.C.s.

Table 1: Interviewees from Local Studies

Description	Number
Secretaries of A.C.s and S.C.s	5
Chairmen of A.C.s and S.C.s	5
Members of A.C.s and S.C.s	1
Asian J.P.s	16
Afro-Caribbean J.P.s	15
White J.P.s	8
Unsuccessful black candidates	7
Asian community representatives	19
Afro-Caribbean community representatives	13
Officers of Community Relations Councils	8
Total	97

Before we proceed with an account of our findings, it is necessary to mention some of the difficulties we encountered during our local studies. In the first place, it was made clear to us by officials of the Lord Chancellor's Department that it was highly unlikely that we would be permitted to observe candidates' interviews for the magistracy or the discussions of interview panels or selection committees. These, we were told, were controlled by A.C.s and were strictly confidential. Most of our information on these crucial aspects of the selection process had to come therefore from the accounts given to us by Advisory or Sub-Committee representatives or past candidates. In some instances we had the impression that the answers we received from the selectors' representatives and from some magistrates were a somewhat 'laundered' version of the selection process. We found out, for example, that after one interview of existing magistrates, the magistrates asked the Clerk to the Justices whether they had said anything which they should not have done. On another occasion the secretary to an Advisory Committee, when being interviewed with three Sub-Committee chairmen gave us a totally different answer to that which he had made when interviewed alone previously. This tendency for interviewees to tell us either what they wanted us to believe or what they thought we wanted to hear was not confined to magistrates and officials.

Whenever possible we did check on what we were told, but the secrecy of the selection process made such checks difficult. Where we have doubts, therefore, about the factual accuracy of information received we have either expressed these doubts in the text or have altogether omitted that information.

In the case of selection officials we were not merely concerned with obtaining factual information, but also in discovering their attitudes towards members of the black communities and their presence on the Bench. Here again, the danger was that they would reveal only what they wanted us to hear. To some extent, however, we were able to counter this by allowing them to talk freely for a fairly long period. Almost all these interviews exceeded one-and-a-half hours and some went on for over two hours during which time they were likely to relax and to make general statements from which we were able through subsequent analysis to detect something of their true attitudes.

One further preliminary note is necessary. As we anticipated, we found considerable variation in the methods of recruitment and selection from one area to another, in the attitudes of the participants to the process, and in the size and nature of the black population. We must emphasise that we did not intend to carry out a detailed comparative study between the different areas. While, therefore, we have tried as far as possible to bring out these differences in the text, we do from time to time make generalisations where we believe these to be justified by the evidence. While these general statements are applicable to all the five areas of our local studies, they may not hold true to the same degree in each.

Chapter 4

THE APPOINTMENTS SYSTEM

'What you get is an institution which is better than any other I know and getting better all the time.'

Lord Hailsham on the magistracy
(interview for ITV's 'The Law Machine', 1983)

The first objective of our research was to find out as much as possible about what is probably the most secretive administrative organisation in Britain — that concerned with the selection and appointment of J.P.s.

We decided not to confine our examination simply to an identification of the sort of individuals and committees responsible for appointments to the Bench and a description of the official roles they play within the system. We wanted rather to uncover, as far as we could, any underlying structures of power and influence that might provide us with some understanding of the make-up of the present magistracy. Why was it that certain types of people tended to be appointed and others rejected? In particular, we wanted to discover whether these structures might affect the number of black people who are appointed to the Bench.

Our research into these issues first took the form of an examination of the remarkably small amount of literature that has been written on the subject of magistrates' selection and appointment. Later we were able to supplement our reading with the information we obtained from our discussions with members of the Lord Chancellor's Office and from our interviews with secretaries and members of Lord Chancellor's Advisory Committees and Sub-Committees which we conducted as part of our local studies.

Politics and the Selection Process

The Lord Chancellor's and the Chancellor of the Duchy of Lancaster's Advisory Committees have the general responsibility of selecting suitable candidates for the magistracy and recommending them for appointment. Since the changes in the country's administrative areas in 1972 the areas of responsibility for each A.C. has corresponded to the administrative divisions of metropolitan and non-metropolitan counties. There are, therefore, 113 A.C.s, ninety-six serving the Lord Chancellor and seventeen, the Duchy of Lancaster.* All the non-metropolitan counties and the larger metropolitan counties include in their respective areas several magistrates' courts and, in order to maintain the local nature of the appointments to the Bench, S.C.s or area panels were established for these counties in 1972. There are 153 S.C.s which interview candidates in their areas. Instead of passing their names directly to the Lord Chancellor, they submit them to the A.C. for approval. Those candidates approved by the A.C. are then recommended to the Lord Chancellor.

H.G. Wells once described the magistracy as having 'the aura of the minor knighthood' (Skyrme, 1979, p.48). Certainly in the past appointment as a Justice of the Peace was seen either as an automatic reward for public or political service or as a formal recognition of status and worth in the community. But the establishment of Lord Chancellor's A.C.s following the Report of the Royal Commission on Justices of the Peace in 1910, the implementation of the recommendations of a second Royal Commission in 1948 and the efforts of successive Lord Chancellors in recent years have succeeded in substantially reducing this element of honour and reward in the appointment of magistrates but not, perhaps, in eliminating it altogether.

The introduction of the A.C. system was an attempt to overcome not only the honour and reward tradition in making people J.P.s, but also the blatant political influence over appointments. Before 1949, however, it failed to have the desired effect because the committees themselves were highly political, often carving up between the major parties the recommendations for appointment which they submitted to the Lord Chancellor (Skyrme, p.52).

According to Sir Thomas Skyrme, who worked as the Secretary of Commissions in the Lord Chancellor's Department, the climax to the conflict between justice (in the form of Lord Chancellors who wanted magistrates to have all the virtues and qualities of judges) and politics (in the form of the main parties, who wanted their supporters on the Bench) came during the post-War Labour

*Reference to the Lord Chancellor and the Lord Chancellor's Department in the remainder of this report will include the Chancellor to the Duchy of Lancaster and his department

24

Government when Lord Jowitt was Lord Chancellor. Jowitt started by resisting all pressure from his party to appoint a large number of Labour supporters to the Bench to balance the prevailing Conservative majority. However, soon after the Royal Commission Report of 1948 he was forced into a compromise. He sent a ministerial directive to A.C.s telling them that, 'The first and most important consideration in the selection and appointment of justices is that the candidate should be personally suitable in point of character, integrity and understanding and should be recognised as such by those among whom they work and live . . .' However, appointment was still not to be simply a matter of picking those who were best able to do the job, for Lord Jowitt then continued,

> . . . it is impractical to disregard political affiliations in making appointments. Once an adequate number of suitable persons is available it is of very great importance (a) that they should be drawn from all sections of the community so as to represent a microcosm or cross-section of all shades of opinion and (b) that there should be no overweighting in favour of any one section . . . The Lord Chancellor finds that political affiliations are a convenient guide to follow but this does not imply that he will only appoint persons who are known to be adherents of a particular party (Skyrme pp.53-4).

Personal suitability and social balance, and not party political affiliations, were, therefore, according to Jowitt, the two essential criteria in appointment. However, party politics continue to play an important part both directly and indirectly in determining who sits on the Bench. As Elizabeth Burney, who recently conducted research into the magistracy, puts it, 'Although party politics is . . . only one of a series of interwoven strands, which contributes to Bench membership, it remains almost everywhere the most consistent one' (p.58).

One does not have to search very far to find the reasons. For a start, political labels are a convenient way of classifying people, an easily observable barometer of the mainstream social opinions. Candidates nominated by the major political parties are unlikely to be 'extremists' or 'trouble-makers'. Secondly, it is political imbalance, rather than any other sort of imbalance, which is likely to provoke the loudest complaints. This is not because these imbalances are more important than others, but because political parties are more highly motivated, have more resources, such as voices in the Parliamentary Chambers, and are more skilful than other groups in pursuing their own interests.

But, as we shall see, the preoccupation with politics, far from aiding diversity of attitudes and backgrounds on the Bench, may actually conflict with Jowitt's aim to draw magistrates from *all* sections of the community, particularly where certain of these sections are not particularly active in mainstream politics.

It is the Lord Chancellor who has the power to appoint and dismiss A.C. and S.C. members and one way in which he today attempts to ensure political balance on the Bench is in his choice of members to sit on these committees. Each such committee now, 'includes a number of recognised supporters of different parties' (Skyrme p.42). The Lord Chancellor even goes to the lengths of checking with party headquarters that these members are in fact known to be party supporters. However, it is a condition of their appointment that they do not 'regard themselves as supporting party interests while exercising their committee duties' (Skyrme p.42) — another compromise, reflecting the conflict between justice and politics.

The Committees and the Local Bench

Whether or not their appointments are politically inspired, most A.C. and S.C. members were drawn from the ranks of magistrates or former magistrates. In fact, in 1982, of the 1,900 or so members of those committees serving the Lord Chancellor, only 163 (8.6 per cent) were neither serving nor retired magistrates.[11] In the area covered by the Duchy of Lancaster, involving twenty-one A.C.s, the number of members who did not serve at that time, or had not served as J.P.s, is as low as six.[12] Our own survey of thirty-five A.C.s and S.C.s revealed that out of 292 committee members, no fewer than 265 (91 per cent) were magistrates. The official justification for this situation is that those with experience of sitting on the Bench are the best people to judge whether or not a candidate would make a good magistrate. However, the obvious, frequently made criticism of this arrangement is that it serves to perpetuate the character of the Bench by ensuring that those appointed will share the values and attitudes of existing magistrates.

Another indication of the close connection between A.C.s and the local Bench is the number of chairmen of the Bench who also take the chair of the A.C. or S.C., and Clerks to the Justices who double as secretaries to Advisory Committees. While we were unable to obtain information on how many S.C.s are chaired by the chairmen of the local Bench, the number of Clerk/secretaries in the ninety-six Lord Chancellor's A.C.s is forty-two (44 per cent).[13]

For S.C.s this figure is even higher with 65 per cent (ninety-seven out of 148) having a Clerk to the Justices as their secretary.[14] Although the secretary has no vote in the committees' decisions as to whom they should recommend, our local research indicated that he or she may nevertheless have a considerable influence over policy and procedure. The secretary is almost invariably consulted on such matters as how to attract nominations or how interviews should be conducted. Moreover, it is to the secretary that all nominations for the Bench are directed. In some cases, this may go no further than simply acting as a post-box for nomination forms and references, but both Elizabeth Burney's (p.74) and our own research indicates that in some cases they may play a much more active and influential role including the interviewing of candidates.

Secrecy and Committee Membership

Another important characteristic of A.C.s and S.C.s is the secrecy surrounding their membership. With the exception of Inner London and, more recently, Essex, which decided to 'go public' and publish the names of their members, and one A.C. where the local MP revealed the names to the press, the identity of the committee members is a closely guarded secret.

The official reasons for such secrecy are to prevent committee members being lobbied and pressurised by prospective candidates and their supporters and to avoid complaints about the membership of committees from the sections of the local population who feel that they are not adequately represented (Skyrme, p.44).

Facts about the membership of committees have, therefore, been hard to come by. We know from past research that while they vary in size, 'most A.C.s have about twelve members and S.C.s about six or eight' (Skyrme, p.42). We know also that in non-metropolitan counties the Lord Lieutenant of the county is almost always appointed chairman of the A.C., but in metropolitan counties the Lord Lieutenant usually co-ordinates the work of the district committees without actually taking the chair (Skyrme p.41). In Inner London the practice in recent years has been to appoint a senior judge as chairman, with Judge West Russell taking over from Lord Denning in 1977. Circuit judges also sit as chairman on two committees outside London, but the usual practice in metropolitan areas is to appoint the chairman of the local Bench to act also as the A.C. chairman.

Although, in theory, the chairman and members of the committees are appointed for six years with half the committee resigning every three years,[15] in practice it is not unknown for them to hold office for twelve years.[16] None of the members of the A.C. receive any payment for their labours and, although they may claim the same loss of earnings allowance as magistrates, few in fact do so[17] (see p.74).

Central and Local Control

The Lord Chancellor does not officially exert control over the way in which the A.C.s or S.C.s conduct their affairs. Each committee is autonomous, deciding, for example, such matters as whether it should advertise to attract nominations and whether all candidates should be interviewed. However, the staff of the Lord Chancellor's Department, and in particular the Secretary and Deputy Secretary of Commissions do offer advice and guidance to the committees.[18] This advice and guidance takes the form not only of ministerial directions and memoranda, but also of visits about once every three years from the Lord Chancellor's staff.

Because of the diversity of procedures it is difficult to generalise about the precise way in which magistrates are selected. Each A.C. has virtually a free hand in how it sets about the task. The only rules that apply everywhere relate to restrictions as to whom may be appointed to the Bench. The most important of these is the geographical qualification: magistrates must reside in (or within fifteen miles of the boundary of) the commission and live or work within the area of the petty sessional division where they sit as magistrates.[19] The single significant statutory disqualification is bankruptcy, but successive Lord Chancellors have made it clear that they are not prepared to consider the following people for the Bench:

a. the spouse, parent, son, daughter, brother or sister of an existing Justice in the same Petty Sessional Division;
b. a serving police officer or a member of the Special Constabulary Forces, or a traffic warden, or the spouse, parent, son, daughter, brother or sister of a police officer if the officer is a member of a police force the area of responsibility of which includes the Petty Sessional Division;
c. a serving member of H.M. Forces;
d. a person who have been convicted of a serious offence or of a series of minor offences;
e. an officer or servant of a magistrates' court in his own Petty Sessional Division;
f. a Member of Parliament, a candidate for election to Parliament who has been formally adopted as a prospective candidate, or a full-time paid party political agent if the Petty Sessional Division area covers any part of the constituency;

28

parties has at least one supporter sitting on every A.C. or S.C., but, as might be expected, like the local Bench, local political parties are often a fruitful source of nominations for the magistracy.[25] Of course, many prominent local politicians are also J.P.s, thus establishing and maintaining close links between Bench, selection committees and local political parties.

What we have not shown in Figure 2, and what would be extremely difficult to demonstrate diagrammatically is the extent to which local voluntary bodies other than political parties may influence the selection process. Organisations such as the Rotary Club, Round Table and Freemasons' Lodges, attracting as they do a membership of mainly business managers and professional people, have in the past proved fertile hunting ground for new recruits to the magistracy. The most notorious example is that of the Rochdale Bench in the mid-seventies, 49 per cent of whose magistrates were Rotarians and 28 per cent Freemasons (Bartlett & Walker, 1973). Once strong ties between Benches and such organisations have been established it is easy to see, from our knowledge of the selection process, how these ties are likely to be perpetuated and strengthened still further. Rotarian or Freemason members of the Bench propose 'suitable' people they have met at Rotary or Lodge functions.

The same development of close ties with the local Bench and a potential influence over the selection process may also apply to Chamber of Commerce, councils of social services and Church bodies, but always not, it seems, to working-class bodies. Indeed, Elizabeth Burney, found in her research that the selectors of magistrates often complained that 'Trade unions nominate their own officials as magistrates, instead of finding ordinary workers to sit on the Bench' (p.13), and were not consequently regarded as particularly useful sources of recruitment. This complaint was echoed by one or two A.C. representatives in our own study.

'Frankly if they [the Labour Party] tend to make nominations at all, it tends to be of the old political hacks, round about their sixtieth birthday.' (Secretary, Harley A.C.)

What then were the conclusions that we were able to draw from the knowledge we acquired of the appointments system? In the first place we were struck by the intimate nature of the system, both in terms of its secrecy and by the way in which considerable power is vested in the hands of very few people. This inner circle consists of the chairman of A.C.s and S.C.s, the secretaries of these committees and three or four officials from the Lord Chancellor's Department. None of them are accountable to anyone other than the Lord Chancellor, yet it was they who between themselves decided who should sit on the selection committees. Moreover, for each committee these decisions, it appeared, were very largely based on the personal judgement of just one person, the chairman, although he might seek the advice of his secretary. Only people personally known to the chairman and, presumably approved of by him, were therefore, likely to be appointed to be members of A.C.s or S.C.s. It was likely, then, that the absence of black people among the chairman's close acquaintances either on the magistrate's Bench or in his other political or social activities would reduce considerably the chances of appointment to selection committees, unless there were strong external pressure to bring members of ethnic minorities into the appointments system. In fact, our survey revealed that out of 292 A.C. and S.C. members there were two Asians, only one of whom came from the Indian sub-continent, and not a single Afro-Caribbean person.

Another possible reason for the seemingly low representation of black people on selection committees was the voluntary basis on which they were run. True to the British tradition members of A.C.s and S.C.s were unpaid for their work, although they were entitled to compensation for loss of earnings at the same rate as magistrates in respect of the time they devoted to their committee work. Few, however, claimed this compensation. This tradition, of course, cuts both ways. While it ensures that those who take on this work do so for 'the right reasons', and not purely for financial gain, it also tends to exclude those people who cannot take time off work or for whom the compensation offered falls far short of their actual loss. As we shall see these same reasons were offered to us by those selecting magistrates as explanations as to why so few black people put themselves forward for the Bench. They could also explain in part the almost total absence of black people on selection committees.

Turning now to actual appointments to the magistracy, our analysis of the structure of the system was able to provide us with some idea of the sort of people who stood the strongest chance of being proposed as magistrates and of receiving the approval of the selection committee.

Applying the principle that 'like attracts like', the most successful candidates for the magistracy would be likely to be people who know one or more members of the existing Bench, preferably J.P.s of some seniority who are known and respected by their colleagues and the Justices' Clerk. They would most probably have come into contact with these magistrates through their work or through voluntary committees or charitable organisations. Involvement in local politics through one of the major political parties would also be a strong positive asset, since we knew that these parties are important, firstly, in ensuring a 'balanced' Bench, secondly, as a source of proposals for the magistracy and, thirdly, as a meeting ground where the candidate might well come into contact with existing magistrates and perhaps with members of the selection committee. Burney's research indeed shows that these factors were certainly important among those white people who were selected as J.P.s. It remained for us to discover whether these same factors applied equally to black magistrates as they appeared to do in respect of white J.P.s.

Chapter 5

FINDING BLACK CANDIDATES

The Appointment of Magistrates
The committees welcome nominations of persons in all walks of life
who are thought to have the qualities and time to serve as Justices
of the Peace. Any person or body may recommend a candidate for
appointment.

(extract from advertisement placed in all national papers by the
Lord Chancellor's Dept and Duchy of Lancaster Office in
November 1983)

The Ideal of Community Justice

We started both our research and this report with a clear idea of the
role black people could be playing in the administration of justice
(see Chapter 2). It concerned the relative and discretionary nature
of many courtroom decisions and the need, therefore, to bring into
the legal system as broad a cross-section as possible of experience,
beliefs and opinions about the sorts of issues which arise in court.
In our ideal of community justice members of the black
communities, be they Asians, Afro-Caribbeans or members of any
community, would have a particular contribution to make in terms
of the perspectives they could bring to the consciousness of the
Bench.

Although there was official concern in the Lord Chancellor's
Department and the Office of the Duchy of Lancaster about the
apparent paucity of black magistrates, the reasons behind this
concern, it soon became clear, were not related to our community-
justice ideal. What bothered them was the public image of the
magistracy. Black people were to be recruited to the Bench, not
because of their potential contribution to justice, but to give the
Bench the appearance of representing the whole community, to
forestall criticism of bias and to retain public confidence.

When later we interviewed representatives of selection
committees in different parts of the country, it was always these
concerns which lay behind any attempt to find black magistrates.
We discuss at some length in chapter ten the preoccupation of
A.C.s with 'balancing the Bench' and its implication for ethnic
minorities. Suffice it to say at present that the motives behind such
recruitment exercises will influence both the sort of black people

the committees look for and the ways in which they set about looking for them.

If our community-justice ideal had been, therefore, the inspiration for the search for black J.P.s, they would have tried to find people whose views on the sort of court issues we have mentioned were close to those expressed by most other members of that black community. To seek these people out, the committee would have gone to 'grass-root' organisations within black community organisations, the temples, the mosques, the Asian and Afro-Caribbean workers' organisations, the clubs, the cultural centres. In practice, however, the local A.C.s and S.C.s, prompted into action by very different motives, set about their task in a very different way.

Before we discuss the results of our research into recruitment and nomination, it is important to mention that although this section of our report is, for the sake of clarity, divided into separate chapters, the process is a continuous one, with each of the various stages in selection interrelating in complex ways. The source of a candidate's nomination and the status of his or her referees may, for example, influence the attitude of the interview panel. The groups or individuals who nominate candidates may be influenced by past failures or successes of their nominees at the hands of the selectors. Similarly, the attitude of A.C. members towards recommending Afro-Caribbean or Asian candidates for appointment may be influenced by their estimation of the performance of other members of these communities on the Bench.

Attitudes Towards Recruitment of Black Magistrates

It was by no means always the case that the selection committees had come to regard the recruitment of black magistrates as a matter of concern. In some areas the black population may have been well represented on the Bench, but our statistical analysis of Benches and the local black population (see Chapter 12) suggests that this was rarely so. In Thorburn, for example, an industrial town with a significant black population and relatively few black magistrates, a member of the A.C. told us that he did not see increasing the number of black magistrates as a 'major concern'. However, he conceded, 'It would be more of a concern if [the city] had a race problem. Then we might have to find a black person to sit on the committee itself.' In this city the recruitment of black magistrates had been undertaken by one member of the A.C. until his recent retirement. The chairman told us that in replacing him no attempt had been made to find someone who might play a similar role. This committee, in common with some others, saw their recruitment job as essentially one of vetting nominees rather than actively going out and looking for new magistrates. We were told, 'It's up to ethnic minorities to put forward names rather than the Advisory Committee to go out and encourage them to do so . . . even if the ethnic minorities are not putting forward names, it's not for Advisory Committee members to do so.'

For many other committees, however, including the remaining four in our local study, the dearth of black magistrates was clearly seen as a problem. Indeed, of the thirty-five committees who completed our questionnaire, nineteen (54 per cent) stated that they had been concerned about not receiving enough applications from black people. As Table 2 shows, all but two of these stated that they had taken some positive steps to encourage black nominations. Six of the seventeen who said that they took positive action stated that they routinely sought contact with local black communities to make them aware of the possibility of applying to join the Bench. There were also another five committees who told us that, while they were not concerned about the numbers of black magistrates, they nevertheless circulated information to local black communities. Thus twenty-two out of thirty-seven committees claimed to have some contact with the local black population.

Only five of the committees responding to our questionnaire stated that they took the initiative of going to black community organisations personally in their efforts to increase the number of black candidates. Once again we found this surprising, but, given the limited time and resources of selection committees and the motive behind the exercise to recruit black magistrates, perhaps we should have been less surprised.

We can perhaps best illustrate the variations in attitude and approach among those selection committees concerned at the low number of black candidates by taking the two extreme examples from our local study.

In Harley the A.C. had been worried for some years that the large Asian, mainly Pakistani, community in the city was considerably under-represented on the Bench. The committee's response was actively to seek out Asian candidates. At first a close informal relationship was established with the Community Relations Council and in particular with the Community Relations Officer, who acted almost as an unofficial A.C. member, passing on the names of likely Asian candidates and informing the committee of their qualities and defects. When he resigned, this close relationship with the local Community Relations Council came abruptly to an end. Shortly afterwards, the Lord Chancellor, presumably on the recommendation of the A.C. chairman and secretary, appointed a fairly junior Asian magistrate to the A.C.. According to the secretary, 'We did feel that if we're having Asians, the committee should have received direct advice on the suitability of Asian candidates from one of their own people.' As we shall see, however, this appointment proved to be something of a mixed blessing so far as attempts to increase the number of Asian candidates were concerned (see p.71).

Table 2: Concern Expressed over Number of Black Candidates and Action Taken: Questionnaire Replies*

	A.C. expressed concern	A.C. did not express concern
	19	14
Sought contact with black communities	17	5
Action taken *(No. of times mentioned)*		
Used 'usual channels'[26]	13	5
Contacted C.R.C. or C.R.O.	7	1
Contacted black J.P.s	3	2
Contacted Afro-Caribbean or Asian organisations	3	2

(*Two A.C.s did not reply to these questions)

Moreover, in order to stimulate interest in the Bench and the magistrates' role among the local Pakistani population, the committee arranged for an article to appear in the local Urdu[27] newspaper and the chairman went to talk at a Sikh temple. When we interviewed the chairman and secretary, we were impressed by the obvious interest they took in the local Asian communities, knowing something of their histories, cultures and intergenerational problems. They told us of their frustration at not being able to understand the politics of the Pakistani community and their failure to find more suitable candidates to recommend for appointment to the Bench, in spite of their not inconsiderable efforts.

In Metropole, on the other hand, the size and diversity of the commission's area, with its several S.C.s, made it extremely difficult for the A.C. to develop the sort of informal contacts that existed to some degree at Harley and which might have enabled it to approach black communities in the search for suitable candidates.

The Metropole Committee was content to rely upon the standard routes for recruitment to the magistracy to pick up Afro-Caribbean and Asian applicants, which it identified as being the main minority groups in the area. Although the committee publicised 'the opportunity to apply for appointment', this did not include contacting Afro-Caribbean or Asian organisations. Publicity included encouraging local authorities in the area to place articles in their own free news-sheets, and asking them to display notices which explained the rudiments of the selection process. Notices for display were also made available to large firms, trade union branches and all the mainstream political parties. When we asked an A.C. representative why the Metropole committee did not contact Afro-Caribbean and Asian organisations, one reason we were given was that the committee feared that such contact might be interpreted as a commitment to appoint magistrates from these organisations and that if an appointment were not made, there would be resentment. However, we cannot understand why this should be more true of Afro-Caribbean and Asian organisations than of other bodies which were contacted.

More revealing perhaps was the committee's view that it should address itself to what it described as 'broadly-based' organisations. These included political parties and Women's Institutes, but not 'immigrant groups' which were seen as seeking to further the interests of their members rather than the interests of the community at large. What was particularly surprising was the fact that the committee did not even write to Community Relations Councils asking for nominations to the Bench. When we pressed the secretary of the A.C. on this matter, he gave the following explanation:

[Community Relations Councils] have taken a positive lead in some areas but can hardly be said in those areas — the couple I have in mind — to be interested in the community. They are interested in a certain branch of the community. The magistracy serves the community, not a particular branch of it.

It also seemed that the A.C. were not impressed by candidates nominated in the past by Community Relations Councils and that this may have influenced their present neglect of these organisations as possible sources for nominations. According to the secretary,

All too frequently Community Relations Council candidates are office holders of the Community Relations Council, who are not necessarily the right kind of person . . . If there are questions as to their motivation, it tends to be that they see themselves as representatives.

Sources of Recommendations

Of those black people whose names went forward to selection committees only three out of the thirty-eight we interviewed were self-nominations. Almost all applications involved the participation — as instigator, proposer or referee — of someone who was either already a J.P. or who was involved in local political activities or both. Moreover, as we shall see in Chapter 12, many of those who were eventually appointed to the Bench were themselves generally the sort of people who were active in what might be described as 'mainstream politics', meaning politics which involved the four major political parties. This does not mean to say that these successful black candidates were not also active in black community organisations, but that in general these activities were not considered sufficient on their own to qualify them for the magistracy.

The view we formed from our local studies was that only rarely did community organisations or groups themselves put forward candidates (see pp.124-8). The chairman and secretary of Harley A.C. told us, for instance, that they had never had any applications from a black community organisation. Only one of six local black organisations we contacted in Tranley district of Metropole County had put forward names and this organisation had suggested only one candidate. In Darley district of the same county the Community Relations Councils had sent out 200 letters to black organisations and prominent local black people. Disappointingly, they received only two replies suggesting possible black candidates.

Our overall impression of the low involvement of community groups and the high level of participation from existing magistrates and local politicians was confirmed by the replies we received from selection committees to our questionnaire, which asked them to identify the sources of their applications from black candidates, and by the replies we received in interviews from candidates and former candidates to questions asking them how they came to be proposed for the Bench. These findings are set out in detail in Table 3.

This table clearly shows that existing magistrates and local politicians were by far the most actively involved groups in finding and recommending black candidates for the Bench. This participation by J.P.s in the nomination process was not, it should be mentioned, confined to black candidates. When we examined the A.C. records in two of our local study areas we found that in one area they had proposed as many as 75 per cent of candidates over the past ten years and over 35 per cent in the other. So far as black candidates are specifically concerned, some committees make a point of using members of the Bench in their efforts to find suitable people. One A.C. representative told us that senior magistrates and other magistrates who belong to or are in close contact with black communities 'are a fertile source of applications'. He added, 'There is a close liaison between the secretary of the committee and a long-serving West Indian magistrate who actively encourages West Indian and Asian candidates to come forward.'

Table 3: Sources of Applications and Recommendations

	Number of times mentioned by A.C. and S.C. in response to question 8 of questionnaire (n = 31) (no response = 4)	Number of times mentioned by candidates as instigator or referee (n = 37)
Magistrates	14	16 ⎫
Magistrates who were also local politicians	(unknown)	13 ⎬ 29
Local politicians and political parties	10	11 ⎭ 24
Community Relations Officers and/or Councils	12	8
Afro-Caribbean or Asian Organisations (incl. temples)	6	4
Trade Unions	5	2
Community organisations (e.g. CAB)	2	—
Employers	2	—
Local Authority Officials	1	1
Other Personal Contacts	6	2

In some areas something of a snowball effect may develop with the appointment of members of black communities to the Bench, encouraging other members of their communities to become candidates. We found some evidence of this happening in Branston in recent years where it seemed that the knowledge that three members of the Afro-Caribbean community had been recently appointed was an incentive for others to let their names go forward.

Yet it should not be imagined that all or even most black J.P.s see themselves as unofficial recruiting officers for the magistracy. Several of those we interviewed had neither encouraged nor seen it as their business to encourage others from their community to apply. One black J.P. from Thorburn, an area where the A.C., as we have seen, showed little concern about the shortage of black candidates, told us, for example, that he had not proposed anyone for the Bench. 'Nobody has asked me my views about it . . . I do not see it as my task going as a scout to scout and look for ethnic minorities to propose to the Bench.' Moreover, some black magistrates who had few contacts with other black people, simply did not know any other members of the minority group to which they belonged, whom they would consider proposing.

Where a political party or a local politician was involved in the black candidate's application, the party concerned was usually Labour.[28] However, there was no consistency from area to area in the level of activity by Constituency Labour Parties or local Labour Councillors in proposing candidates for the Bench nor in the use made by the A.C. of the Labour Party as a potential source of black applicants. In Harley, for example, the A.C. secretary told us that the Labour Party 'tend to put forward committee resolutions as to who should go on the Bench which, frankly, tend to be people who are too old and too political. In other words, it tends to be a reward for long service to the Labour Party.'

An Asian community leader also mentioned that in fact Harley Labour Party did not propose Asian candidates. 'Asians do not become members of the Labour Party and the Labour Party does not put their names forward for various positions.'

In Fridham District of Metropole County, in contrast, three of the four Asian magistrates, and one of the unsuccessful candidates interviewed had been proposed by the Labour Party and in Thorburn, every black member of the Bench had been put forward by the Labour Party. In fact it was one particular Labour member of the A.C. who had been responsible for all these applications.

Although there is no doubt that one of the reasons that there were so few successful black candidates was that black community groups so rarely chose to put forward candidates, it should also be emphasised that, even if they had done so, it is very unlikely that their nominees would have been selected without some evidence that they had involved themselves in some mainstream political activity or some public or charitable service known and understood by the selectors. Several of the selectors we interviewed gave as a reason for rejecting black candidates nominated exclusively by black groups the fact that these candidates were not sufficiently experienced in the problems of society beyond the world of the minority group to which they belonged.

Another reason given for rejecting such candidates was that to favour one particular black organisation might upset the remainder of the community, so defeating the purpose of the exercise which was, apparently, to appoint someone who had earned the respect of their whole community. As the Harley Secretary told us, 'We find their [Pakistani] politics a complete tangle . . . But the difficulty is that almost any person that is put forward is unacceptable in a very extreme way to almost three-quarters of their own community.'

Since the same criterion of acceptability is not applied to white candidates, it was difficult to interpret this attitude except in terms of racial discrimination against black people. This is an issue which we shall take up again in our general discussion of discrimination and prejudice. (See Chapter 11.)

One might have thought that the most obvious source of black candidates for the magistracy would have been the national network of Community Relations Councils with their ability to provide local knowledge on likely candidates from the black community, encouragement to black people to put their names forward and the opportunity for potential black candidates to meet people involved in local 'mainstream' community activities who would be prepared to sponsor them as proposer or referee. But though some C.R.C.s did serve this purpose, their participation in the selection process was by no means as great as one might have expected. Much depended upon the attitude of the Community Relations Officer and members of the C.R.C. towards the magistracy and the selection system (see pp.126-8), and also, as we have seen from the example of Metropole County, on the way in which the selectors or the secretary of the selection committee viewed the local C.R.C. There would be little or no participation of the C.R.C. in the search for black magistrates in an area where the organisation was regarded as subversive or antipathetic to the role of the magistrates' court. As Table 3 shows, only twelve out of the thirty-one selection committees which replied to the relevant question mentioned the Community Relations Officer or Council as a source of applications for the Bench. We discuss possible reasons for the negative attitude of some C.R.C.s to the selection process in Chapter Thirteen.

Chapter 6

SIFTING THE CANDIDATES

What happens to black candidates after their names are put forward depends upon the A.C. responsible for selection in the commission area concerned. There are considerable variations from area to area, for, apart from the expectation that every person recommended to the Lord Chancellor for appointment should have been interviewed, there is no attempt by the Lord Chancellor's Office to impose uniformity within the selection process.

Although the Lord Chancellor's Office has overall responsibility for and control over the selection process, including the appointment of A.C. and S.C. members, it does not undertake any regulation or control over the way in which the selection committees carry out their day-to-day business, preferring to act in a purely advisory capacity. In practice, this means that each A.C. chooses its own selection methods and these choices tend in most commission areas to be made by the chairman and secretary of the A.C.. Even in the five areas of our local study, therefore, there were substantial differences in the ways in which the selection committees set about their task, as Table 4 indicates.

It is important at this stage to say something about the way in which pre-interview information about the candidate was collected and placed before the committee members. As we have already mentioned, each candidate completes an application form giving personal information including political views and any previous criminal convictions (motoring offences included) (see Appendix V). This form also asks for the names of two people recommending the candidate. Then, unless the candidate is obviously ineligible to sit as a magistrate through age, address or being within one or other of the categories of people excluded by the Lord Chancellor (see pp.28-9), the A.C. secretary will in almost every case write to the referees asking them for their opinion of the candidate's suitability.

Apart from references, there are considerable variations in the way in which other information is gathered. In Harley for example, representatives of the A.C. told us that they were able to make use of their contacts within the local Asian community to discover more about the candidate, although the secretary admitted that it was 'more difficult (than in the past) to check on the background, now that we've lost contact with the Community Relations

Council'. Other possible contacts for the purposes of 'discreet enquiries' by the Harley committee include, as might be expected, existing magistrates and local political parties. The questions asked might cover any aspect of the candidate's life — his financial situation, domestic arrangements, any useful knowledge in fact which the contact was able to provide. Enquiries, according to the Harley secretary, may take the form of an open question such as, 'I understand that X has applied for the magistracy. How do you think he would do at that?' The trusted contact need not even have first-hand knowledge of the candidate. 'It need not necessarily be personal contact with individuals . . . it could be somebody who knows somebody.' (Secretary, Branston A.C.)

Table 4: Procedures Adopted by Advisory Committees and Sub-Committees

Committee	Enquiries and Investigations	Interviewed	Interview Panel
Branston City S.C.	Yes	Short-list	S.C. chairman + 2 or 3 other S.C. members. secretary present
Harley A.C.	Yes	All eligible candidates	A.C. chairman + 2 committee members. secretary not present.
Meadowport A.C.	References taken up. (No other information available.)	All eligible candidates.	All 8 members of A.C. secretary present.
Metropole County A.C.	(No firm information available)	All eligible candidates	All members of 1 of 4 S.C.s each of which has 5 or 6 members. secretary or deputy present.
Thorburn S.C. (Southern County A.C.)	Yes	Short-list	Any 3 of 6 S.C. members. secretary not present.

A similar system of 'discreet enquiries' operated at Branston A.C.. In neither area did the members of the A.C. or the secretary have the time or the resources to check with any thoroughness the information they obtained. The policy was rather to ensure that the contact was 'reliable'. 'You've got to be sure of whom you ask,' one Branston City S.C. member told us.

Branston A.C. also used the secretary to conduct informal interviews of candidates who were not personally known to members of the committee. According to the secretary, he tended to undertake such preliminary interviews with every black candidate (and some white) who sent in an application form, because, 'It's difficult to get them of the right calibre, therefore we cannot afford to leave any stone unturned'. The secretary would then report back to the committee which would decide on the basis of written information and his impressions of the candidate whether that particular candidate should be formally interviewed. Although those black candidates interviewed by the secretary found him a 'nice person' and described their preliminary interviews as 'informal', 'friendly' and 'helpful', the role played by the secretary must be questioned. As secretary he is not a member of the A.C. or S.C. and should, therefore, have no part in the decision-making process. Yet he told us that, while applying 'no particular criteria', he tried to 'pick out' the ones to interview informally whom he thought 'might be more likely than others'. While we accept that his intention was to assist the committee by reducing their work-load, it was impossible not to conclude that his influence over the decision as to who should be short-listed was likely to be considerable. We also take the view that the secretary's report and the way this was presented to members of the interview panels could well affect the latter's perception of the candidate and their assessment of his or her interview performance.

This absence of conformity to specified standards and the lack of any effective controls to ensure that the minimum requirements of procedural justice were respected, could well have prejudiced the chances of some black candidates. Short-listing of candidates was openly admitted at Branston and also took place at Harley. (Although we were assured by representatives of the Harley committee that the aim was to interview all candidates, our examination of the application records clearly showed that this aim had not yet been realised.) In fact, three Asian candidates in Branston and six in Harley were rejected without interview. When we drew this to the attention of the secretary of Branston S.C., he replied that one of these Asian candidates was a self-nomination whose application form contained no indication of public-service experience, while another was considered rather too young at thirty-one years old. This was somewhat surprising, as the records also indicated that a white candidate of twenty-nine years old had in fact been interviewed and appointed.

It may be that all nine of these rejected candidates would have been found unsuitable even if they had been given an interview, but it is also possible that the selectors may have discovered much more positive information about the candidate than appeared on the application form or than they were able to obtain from their 'discreet enquiries'. Indeed, those A.C.s which interviewed or claimed to interview every candidate spoke out strongly against any form of preliminary sifting other than eliminating those who were disqualified under the Lord Chancellor's criteria (see p.28-9).

It is an unnecessary restriction in the opportunity for candidates to present themselves . . . not everybody who is good can actually write application forms to convince you that they're good.

(Secretary, Metropole A.C.)

All are interviewed, even if you have some area of doubt . . . Everyone is entitled to receive an interview.

(Chairman, Harley A.C.)

Another objection to short-listing was how arbitrary it was. If any detailed short-listing procedures or any specific criteria existed, these were never made clear to us. It seemed to us that there was every opportunity for bias to creep in, a criticism which had been anticipated by the Meadowport A.C. secretary who argued that all candidates should be interviewed, because, 'it protects the committee from accusations of political bias in the papers sift'. Indeed, in Thorburn short-listing seemed to be based on little more than the personal knowledge some A.C. members may have had of particular candidates. A candidate could be eliminated purely as the result of an opinion expressed by a single committee member. 'The candidate is often known by a member of the committee and if he says a person is unsuitable, the committee usually go along with that.' (Secretary, South County A.C. [responsible for Thorburn])

We were unable to discover whether any black candidate suffered this particular fate, but through enquiries made in our local studies we reached the general conclusion that both Afro-Caribbean and Asian candidates were likely to be handicapped by too little positive, rather than by too much negative information. In this respect black candidates were in a similar position to white manual workers in that neither tended to be known among the contacts who provided information to the selection committees, simply because they were often not involved in the sort of activities where they were likely to meet such trusted informants. According

50

to the secretary of Branston S.C., 'If a person's involved in politics or other bodies, it's much easier to check him out.' One effect of this dearth of positive information was that it placed additional emphasis on interview performance for those candidates who survived the initial sifting.

Chapter 7

INTERVIEWING

Before examining the way in which black candidates were interviewed, we believe it would be useful to say a few words about selection interviews in general, since a considerable amount has been written on the subject by psychologists and personnel managers.

Although there is much disagreement about the effectiveness of interviews in predicting which candidates are suitable for the job, all writers on the subject are agreed that good interviewing is a skilled business which requires some specialised training or, at the very least, some theoretical knowledge of the interpersonal processes involved. It is agreed that it is good practice that selectors should identify and agree among themselves the qualities that the job requires and what sort of information they need from the candidate to ascertain whether he or she has these qualities. There is also general agreement among these writers that for most jobs the interview, on its own, cannot possibly test whether the candidate is suitable and that selectors should be aware of these limitations. The absence of any interview-skills training combined with failure to specify the qualities sought or to recognise the limitations of interviewing can lead to what one writer has described as 'abominable results' with 'an untrained employer talking generalities about a job he has not analysed' (Plumbley, 1974, p.136). It may also result in the interviewee being compared with some vague notion of what a good candidate ought to be like or with the performance of the last candidate interviewed.

Another cause of inefficient interviewing and ineffective selection is inaccurate person perception. This involves the selectors interpreting the candidate's interview in ways which give a false impression of his or her suitability for the job. Unless interviewers are aware of these difficulties and take conscious steps to counter them, they will tend to make use of those rough-and-ready methods of assessing people which all of us use in our everyday contacts with others. The most common of these is stereotyping, that is 'the tendency to see people as examples of personality types and to attribute all characteristics of that type to a particular individual' (Ribeaux and Poppleton, 1978, p.241; Brigham 1971). The prejudices of the interviewer may give rise to inaccurate interpretations of the interviewee's behaviour or abilities based upon generalisations arising for example from his or her colour, mode of dress, accent, class or occupation. Such stereotyping may well be compounded by bias in favour of candidates who share features in common with the interviewer and against those whose reactions and opinions run counter to his own. According to one writer on the subject, 'judgement can be warped in this way without the interviewer being conscious of it' (Plumbley, p.145).

The unskilled interviewer may also fail to give candidates an opportunity to show what sort of skills, experience and knowledge they have, by making the candidate feel threatened or uncomfortable by interrupting, asking catch questions or behaving in a provocative or aggressive manner towards him or her. Even where the selector strives to put the candidate at ease and create a relaxed atmosphere, lack of skill in questioning may defeat any attempts to obtain useful information. Inexpert questions include those which require only one word answers or leading questions beginning with, for instance, 'I don't suppose . . .' 'Presumably . . .' or 'I expect . . .' and which therefore suggest their own answers or 'may force the candidate to appear to disagree with his questions or to acquiesce for fear of giving offence' (Rodger, 1975, p.158). Less obviously, and one of the commonest faults among weak interviewers according to one commentator, are questions which neglect the distinction between skill and enthusiasm.

To regard a candidate's statement that he is fond of (likes, enjoys, or is in some way keen about) something as equivalent to a claim that he is good at it is a mistake that has been responsible for a great deal of thoroughly bad selection . . . (Rodger, p.158)

In our discussions with officials of the Lord Chancellor's Department, it became clear that they had given some thought in the past to these problems. They had, with the help of personnel selection experts, explored the possibility of devising an aptitude test as an aid to Advisory Committees in the selection of magistrates. However, this project ran into difficulties when it came to translating such concepts as 'the judicial mind', 'commonsense' and 'a balanced approach' into specific skills or personality traits which could be accurately tested. As a result these plans for an aptitude test and any attempt to define with any precision the skills involved in a magistrate's work were dropped.

Instead, the Lord Chancellor's officials have preferred to concentrate their attention upon the interview. To this end in 1977 the Secretary of Commissions distributed to all A.C.s a document entitled *Candidates for the Magistracy: Notes on Interview Procedure*. This was revised in 1980 and it is this revised edition that we have set out in Appendix V. This document consists of eighteen *Notes* from the Assistant Secretary of Commissions followed by three examples of interview guides used by different, unnamed A.C.s.

The first point that anyone knowledgeable about personnel selection would certainly make is that nowhere in these *Notes* is any attempt made to set out the ways in which selectors should set about determining whether a candidate possesses skills and personal qualities required of a magistrate except in the most vague and general terms. Note 8 refers to suitability 'in point of character, integrity and understanding' and of 'the judicial mind', but when it comes to assessing people for these qualities, all the interviewers are told is that,

> persons known to have strong political, religious or other opinions . . . should be carefully scrutinised for the presence or absence of a judicial mind, which may be defined as the capacity to be aware that their personal views may be a potential danger to their impartiality and their willingness and ability to overcome this danger.

One wonders just how the interviewer is supposed to identify this 'capacity to be aware . . .' and 'willingness and ability to overcome . . .'

In the interview guide marked 'A' there appears a list of desirable and undesirable qualities and, while these seem sensible enough, they still place a heavy burden of interpretation on the interviewer both in terms of the meaning of the qualities and in relating the performance of the candidate to the five-point scale. One wonders once again just how a formal interview, however skilfully conducted, is going to provide accurate information on a candidate's ability to make judgements or on his patience and ability to listen. Will a candidate who appears uncertain and is slow to respond in interview necessarily make a poor magistrate in court? The same critical comments could be directed against interview guide 'C' which is described by the Assistant Secretary of Commissions in note 13 as 'a very good assessment form'.

The one major criticism that we would wish to make about these *Notes on Interview Procedure* is that, like so much else relating to the selection of magistrates, there seems to be a preoccupation with form at the expense of any real consideration of the quality and fairness of the decision-making. The problems of interviewer stereotyping, bias and prejudice are not even mentioned. (Ironically, it is only prejudice in the candidate which receives attention.) Nor is any mention made of the effects of stress upon a candidate's interview performance, the assumption being that performance in interview is identical to what one might expect of the candidate if he or she were to sit on the Bench. None of the limitations of formal interviews are discussed nor the obvious difficulties in assessing skills and personality on limited information. This does not mean that the selectors themselves are ignorant of these matters, but their awareness, where it exists, comes from other sources than the Lord Chancellor's Department. Judging from the *Notes,* the officials from this Department seem far more concerned with the possibility of the candidate or his family having criminal convictions or being a target for public criticism and with keeping the identity of the interview panel members confidential, than with issues of interpersonal behaviour, person-perception and decision-making.

We should mention once again the lack of support from these officials for our request to observe selection interviews in progress. Our information on interviewing is, thus, of necessity, based on accounts given to us by representatives of A.C.s and S.C.s and from interviews with magistrates and unsuccessful candidates. However, even if we had been allowed to observe the selection panels at work, any information we obtained would have been unlikely to alter our general conclusion concerning interviews. This is that they are being used for a purpose which they are for the most part incapable of fulfilling, namely to assess which of the candidates are going to make good magistrates.

As we shall see, some of the selection panels tried to overcome the fundamental limitations of formal interviews by trying to turn the interview into a sort of aptitude test, giving candidates hypothetical courtroom problems to solve. Yet there is no reason to believe that the candidates would respond in the same way in the court faced with real decision-making as they did in interview, where at least the more perceptive among them would have tried to give answers they believed would be acceptable to the panel members.

It would be a mistake, however, to see the interview in isolation from the rest of the selection process. All candidates, as we have seen, complete a 'particulars' form (see Appendix V) and, as we have already described, many A.C.s and S.C.s carry out behind-the-scenes investigations before the interview takes place. Interviewers may, therefore, have in front of them at the interview, not only particulars of the candidate's age, job, health, political views and criminal record, but also the opinions and beliefs of others about the candidate's character and suitability. What part this information plays in the selection process is a matter of speculation. If the A.C. and S.C. representatives whom we interviewed are to be believed on this issue, then, for the vast majority of candidates, it is the impression that they give in the interview which is the crucial factor in deciding whether or not they are selected. However, we have the impression that not all the officials to whom we spoke had given adequate thought to the effect of prior information upon the way the candidate is perceived in interview and/or its effect on the decision-making strategies of the interviewers.

According to one study carried out on the effect of different factors on selectors' decisions in job interviews, most interviewers would have made the same decision after four minutes as they would have made at the end of the fifteen-minute interview (see Reading, 1977). The psychologist who carried out this study suggests that a tendency to oversimplify and exaggerate consistencies leads to a 'set' or orientation during the interview. Although he found that in selection interviews the general set is towards caution, this did not operate in an identical manner towards all candidates. Much depended upon prior information and on first impressions. He showed that initial ratings of candidates obtained simply on the basis of the application form correlated highly with the final rating after interview (see Ribeaux and Poppleton, p.242). Another study found that prior information combined with first impressions accounted for no less than 85 per cent of the final results and with 89 per cent of the rejections (see Reading, p.38).

Although it may not be valid to generalise from one or two studies to all interviews and all interviewers, the tendency of interviewers to form a view of the candidate before or at the start of the interview and to use the interview to seek confirmation for this original impression is a sufficiently common phenomenon for us to accept that such a process frequently occurs in selection interviews, particularly where the interviewers are not trained and might not, therefore, be conscious of their decision-making strategies.

The amount of prior information known about each candidate depends, as we have seen, largely upon the investigations of the A.C. or S.C. and this varies considerably from area to area. Yet it is also related to differences between individual candidates. Selection committees are likely to have considerable information about candidates who, for example, sit on committees with existing magistrates, are active in local politics or are deeply involved in community organisations. For these candidates there is good reason to believe from the evidence of studies on interviewing, that their selection or rejection might depend more upon the nature of this prior information and the immediate impression that they make on selectors than upon what happens during the course of the interview. Those candidates about whom very little is known, on the other hand, can expect their interview to be used by selectors as an information-gathering exercise. In these cases the information obtained and the way it was presented by the candidate are likely to be more important factors in the final outcome.

Variations in the amount of information about candidates was not the only difference between interviews carried out in different areas. Our local study also found different approaches among officials as to how many people should conduct the interview, as we indicated in Table 4 on page 48. While Branston and Thorburn used only three or four interviewers, candidates in Meadowport and Metropole found themselves facing the full A.C. or S.C. (up to eight people in one of our local study areas).

Clearly, there is a conflict here between the principle of allowing all committee members to see all candidates and have an equal say in their selection and the demands of effective interviewing. According to the author of *Recruitment and Selection,* published by the Institute of Personnel Management, 'selection boards comprising more than five assessors are often little more than a convenient vehicle for introducing the final candidate(s) to the full committee (Plumbley, p.149). In this author's view, even panels of three to five assessors, while possibly increasing impressiveness and formality and setting uniform standards of judgement, will lose most of their potential advantage over one-to-one interviews or interviews by two assessors, 'unless all the assessors are highly trained and adhere to their allocated roles' (p.149). He implies that panel interviews by untrained assessors run the risk of reducing flexibility and inhibiting the establishment of rapport and suggests that candidates faced with such panels 'may be over-awed or reluctant to talk freely on personal matters', so that 'only the formal behaviour of candidates is observed'.

Further evidence on the limitations of panel interviews comes from Alec Rodger, a psychologist who has studied and written extensively on the problems of personnel selection. He maintains that '[the] usefulness of a board interview may depend a good deal on the competence of the chairman and the good sense of the board members. A promising board interview can be ruined by a member who does not appreciate the line of questioning being pursued by one of his fellow-members and who interrupts with irrelevancies.'

In fact, during the course of our study, an A.C. representative told us just how inept members of magistrates' interview panels could be. He said that there is one interviewer who insists on asking each candidate the direct question: 'Are you prejudiced against coloured or black people?' Not only does this question fail to elicit anything but a firmly negative answer, it also effectively prevents any exploration by other interviewers of the candidate's possible prejudices by more subtle and more revealing ways.

Another way in which selection processes in our study areas differed was in the style of interviewing and the strategies employed. Some selectors favour the 'cosy chat' approach.

> It's in that area [questioning on current issues] that you find the general commonsense approach and it's from that that you get your main understanding of the person and what they're going to do in the future . . . It's more a vehicle for getting them talking, defining what their points of interest are and getting them talking about it, seeing how sensible they are about it.
>
> (Secretary A.C., Branston)

Others, by contrast, preferred shock tactics as a way of making candidates reveal their true colours. 'The [unexpected] question . . . produces an immediate natural reaction, so that in interview the real man or the real woman comes through.' (A.C. Secretary, Meadowport)

One chairman, according to reports we received from candidates, sometimes picked an argument with interviewees by making some remark which was clearly intended to be provocative (see p.61). All the selection officials we spoke to told us that they used hypothetical examples in order to ascertain candidates' views or to place them in the kind of situation of conflict which they might face in court, where their self-interest or political or community loyalties might be at odds with their duties as magistrates. Trade union officials might, for instance, be asked whether they would send to prison pickets who attacked the police, or the proprietor of a shop might be questioned on his views on the punishment of a shoplifter who appeared before him in the dock.

An A.C. responsible for one of the areas covered by our local study has distributed a circular on interview procedure to its S.C.s (see Appendix V). This sets out the sort of questions which the chairman of these S.C.s might well put to candidates. They include:

> Why would you like to be a magistrate, and why do you think you would make a good magistrate?
>
> Have you any misgivings about judging people, convicting them and imposing penalties upon them?
>
> Have you ever visited a magistrates' court or any other court?
>
> Do you have any views on sentencing and how various offences should be dealt with?
>
> How do you feel about the way the law affects the motorist?
>
> Would you comment on the cause and possible cure of football hooliganism?

58

All the A.C. and S.C. representatives to whom we spoke were united in the belief that the interview was an indispensible part of the selection process. There was, however, some variation in the amount of weight placed on interview performance. On the one hand there were those who regarded interviewing as a wholly reliable method of assessing a candidate's suitability for the Bench. 'It [the interview] carries total weight. In effect it's a secret court, but it's a very good one' (Secretary, A.C., Harley). Others had some reservations about interviews as a way of determining a candidate's worth, not because the interviewer might lack the necessary skills in questioning and assessing, but on account of the ability of some candidates to pull the wool over the eyes of the selectors. 'The system has its limitations . . . People can presumably act at the interview . . . Difficult to know about the person until they're appointed' (Secretary, A.C., Metropole County). One A.C. secretary commented that there were 'slick interviewees'. 'Word does get around amongst certain groups about the nature of the interview and so on and they come prepared in a way . . . When you see them performing on the Bench, you realise you were wrong.' He counselled his committee 'not to place too much reliance on the interview performance alone.'

Yet, we must emphasise that such reservations did not detract from the general feeling of confidence among selectors in all five areas we visited that interviewing was a thoroughly effective method of discovering whether a person would make a good magistrate. Some selectors repeated the phrase, 'a 90 per cent success rate', which we had first heard from an official in the Lord Chancellor's Department, referring to the fact that of those appointed only about 10 per cent subsequently left the magistracy before retirement age. This figure was cited as evidence of the efficiency of a selection process based largely on interview assessments, for, according to the logic of some selectors, it showed that they were indeed able to pick out those who would make good magistrates.

This confidence contrasts markedly with the continuing controversy among psychologists and personnel managers about the value and reliability of interviews, and particularly panel interviews, in job selection (Bayne, 1977). From our examination of this literature, it is clear that, despite varying views on the subject of the efficiency of interviews, there is agreement among researchers and commentators on the need for training in interview skills as a prerequisite to the successful eliciting of information and reliable assessment. Yet it was often put to us by A.C. and S.C. representatives in the course of our research that selection for the magistracy was very different from job selection, because candidates were being chosen for their attitudes and character rather than for any specific skills or knowledge. Thus, selection for the magistracy, we were led to believe, is much more of an intuitive process. One S.C. secretary went so far as to claim that the members of interview panels were expert in spotting 'the extremist' or those dogmatic people who 'would not enforce a law properly which does not accord with their views'. 'You spot them through experience,' he told us. 'The gut reaction,' added the chairman of the committee.

Interviewing Black Candidates

In our questions to the A.C. and S.C. representatives we asked specifically about how black candidates fared at interview. Our intention was to find out if there were any aspects of the interviews which might put black people at a disadvantage. This line of questioning gave rise to a number of spontaneous comments about the supposed characteristics of Asians and Afro-Caribbeans. One A.C. chairman told us that Asians tend to be 'arrogant' at their interview; while the A.C. secretary of a different commission area commented, also about Asian candidates, 'They tend to give the impression that they are not expecting to succeed or one gets the reverse situation, that they are rather pompous to the extent that they cannot understand why they should not be accepted'. The representatives who mentioned these supposed racial and cultural characteristics also made it clear to us that they made an effort to take them into account in assessing a candidate's suitability. One A.C. secretary, for example, assured us that he always reminds his selection interviewers that they should 'have regard to West Indian and Asian cultural background in the assessment of them at interview. You expect the volatile and excitable West Indian to come across as volatile and excitable.' According to the secretary of another A.C., however, the basic traits of West Indians are 'slow speaking and having slow reactions'. He went on to describe a particular black candidate's interview: 'I remember his interview vividly. He was stuttering and stammering all the way through it. But that's the way they are sometimes, and nonetheless, we were very impressed by him, his degree of involvement and his concern for people . . . Certainly his manner was in no way prejudicial.'

Some of the generalisations made about black candidates had serious implications for selection in that they related to attitudes towards justice and judicial decision-making. Thus the chairman of one A.C. believed that Asians had a different attitude from others which might prevent them from seeing issues in an objective way.

This, apparently, might lead them to judge a case according to considerations of social justice rather than on the evidence and according to the strict letter of the law. We should add that this view was expressed in an area where the Pakistani community was markedly under-represented on the Bench. Yet we have no doubt that these selection officials would have protested most vehemently had we suggested to them that they were in any way racially prejudiced or that their responses to black candidates were based upon racial stereotypes.

There was also some evidence from our local studies that certain selection committees could on occasions treat black candidates differently to whites during interview. One A.C. secretary told us, for example, how Asians 'usually have to be probed further, because, particularly from the Indian community . . . one of their attitudes is that they ought to respond to the enquirer in the way that the enquirer wants to be responded to.' Moreover, the belief that Pakistani candidates tend, more than others, to see themselves as being 'representatives of their community' led to specific questions on this issue being asked predominantly of Pakistani candidates (see pp.82-3).

Some evidence for differential treatment during interviews also came from the black candidates themselves. A small number, including some successful candidates, were angry about their treatment. One told us how the chairman of the selection panel had made critical remarks about Rastafarians in order apparently to provoke him into an argument. Another complained that he was asked whether he was concerned about the possibility of members of the 'West Indian' community 'putting bricks through his window' if they were unhappy about the decisions of the magistrates' court. A question, he remarked, which would never have been asked of a white candidate.

Generally, however, black candidates did not perceive the interview as being unfair or offensive. While it should be remembered that almost all the former candidates who spoke to us had been successful, even among those who failed to be appointed, critical comments were few and far between. Most candidates said that they had no idea what to expect before the interview began and had therefore not prepared themselves in any way. Their accounts of their interviews varied considerably both individually and according to the A.C. concerned. One, for example, an Afro-Caribbean skilled manual worker told us that he had the impression that 'they were bending over backwards' to get him on the Bench. Others were subjected to thorough questioning, but we have no evidence that black candidates were treated any differently than white in this respect.

As we have seen, one device frequently used by interview panels was to put hypothetical situations to candidates. Candidates did not require any previous detailed knowledge of the law, but this interview strategy may well have given an advantage to those candidates who were familiar with such judicial concepts as the need to enforce the law whatever one's personal views might be about its rightness or wrongness, or the need to impose exemplary sentences regardless of personal sympathies. One such hypothetical situation mentioned by two black candidates whom we interviewed struck us as requiring a familiarity with group or corporate decision making. They asked them how they would react if they found themselves disagreeing with the decision of their colleagues on the Bench. It is perhaps significant that of these two black candidates, the one, who replied that he would 'write a minority report', was eventually appointed, while the other, who said that he would make his objections known in open court, was rejected. It is worth mentioning that this latter candidate also told the interviewers that he believed the police should be prosecuted for perjury when they tell lies from the witness box.

A final point on the interviewing of black candidates concerns the use of interviews to test language ability. Most of the A.C. and S.C. representatives to whom we spoke indicated that competence in English was an important criterion in the selection of J.P.s. One, for example, told us that, 'The Advisory Committees are bound to have regard to the fact that this man at some stage will have to say "You're going to prison for three months".' It was, therefore, essential that they should speak as well as understand the English language. Moreover, all these representatives saw the interview as being the forum where a candidate's competence in English should be tested. According to one A.C. secretary, the committee took the view that if a candidate cannot make himself or herself understood in the context of the interview, that person will have difficulty in absorbing proceedings in court and will not, therefore, be able to play a full part in the work of the Bench. Since magistrates these days frequently have to read reports, particularly social enquiry reports, before sentencing, the selectors to whom we spoke also believed that an ability to read and absorb written English was an essential requirement for a J.P. This, however, created problems, since neither the pre-interview enquiries nor the interview itself contained any comprehension test of written English. Interviewers were therefore reduced to asking candidates such direct questions as, 'Are you able to read English quickly?', although one S.C. chairman told us that he was too embarrassed to interrogate candidates in this way.

The language requirement clearly caused particular problems for

Asian candidates for whom English was a second language. One Asian magistrate told us that there was a risk of selectors being misled by a candidate's lack of confidence in English into believing that he or she was not competent to make judicial decisions.

> . . . The person who waffles about and is not able to express himself totally clearly is not a fool inside . . . Being on the Bench is not a matter of making speeches as in the council chamber. It is a matter, you see, of a bent of mind, a bent of mind that can judge situations in a balanced, rational way. My suspicion is that a lot of candidates who are put forward from the Asian community fall because of that handicap . . .

This magistrate also drew our attention to the fact that a candidate's general interview performance could be affected by his or her language ability. '. . . I think that language is a very important factor, because it is the medium in which one projects one's personality at the interview'.

A selection system which places so much emphasis on interview performance will, therefore, necessarily place at a disadvantage those candidates who lack confidence in their use of English, particularly where the interviews are formal in nature and undertaken by a panel of several interviewers. Moreover, we were not convinced by assurances from several A.C. and S.C. representatives that they compensate for any limitations in an Asian candidate's powers of self-expression in English by going out of their way to help him or her during the interview, for such help, however well intentioned, inevitably draws attention to the candidate's disabilities. The question as to whether the requirement of linguistic competence and the demands of confident self-expression imposed by the formal interview are in fact fair tests of a candidate's likely performance as a magistrate in court is a matter which we shall take up in our discussion of discrimination (see Chapter 11).

Chapter 8

SUITABILITY

> *The first and much the most important consideration in selecting Justices of the Peace is that they should be personally suitable in character, integrity and understanding for the important work which they have to perform, and that they should be generally recognised as such among those with whom they live and work. ('The Appointment and Duties of Justices of the Peace in England and Wales', 1976, Central Office of Information)*

We fully recognise that there are no easy answers to the question: 'Who is suitable to judge others?' and that the task of the A.C.s is extremely difficult and complex. As a preliminary exercise, therefore, we asked ourselves this question to see if it were possible to come up with any objective criteria which could be used to eliminate certain categories of people from the magistracy.

We decided immediately that we would want all J.P.s to be able rapidly to grasp the sense of the sort of written and oral information that they would have to deal with in court. This would exclude all illiterate and semi-literate people and all those who did not have a sufficient understanding of oral English. It would also rule out people who suffered serious hearing and sight infirmities which made it difficult for them to cope with oral or written information. We also agreed that people who experienced serious difficulties in expressing themselves in English should be excluded. The reason for this was not that we expected all magistrates to speak the Queen's English in court with the fluency of a High Court judge. It related rather to what happens outside the courtroom during the bench's deliberations. We thought it necessary for any magistrate to be free from any obvious handicap when debating with his or her colleagues guilt or innocence, the severity of the sentence, or any other of the decisions which J.P.s are obliged to make.

After this initial agreement, our attempt to identify excluding factors became more problematic. We agreed that we would not want to see on the magistrates' Bench people whose beliefs were so blindly held that they prevented them from approaching each case with an 'open mind', but at the same time we knew that nobody is entirely without prejudice. It was therefore a question of degree. What, we decided, we wanted to avoid was the possibility of people on the Bench whose prejudices, of any kind, so influence their judgement that they would be likely actually to distort what they saw or heard in order to obtain a decision of the court which reflected their own biases. We tried in vain to go further and devise other objective criteria. It was easy enough to list the sort of people we personally would not want to see as magistrates, but in no way were our views either consensual or objective. We tended rather to exclude those people whose attitudes towards police evidence, sentencing, state intervention in the family etc. did not conform with our own.

As well as bringing home to us just how difficult was the task of the selectors sitting on A.C.s and S.C.s, this exercise also showed us that once one has excluded the obviously incompetent and those unwilling to listen to evidence with an open mind, it is impossible to assess suitability without relying upon personal beliefs and values. What is more, when we varied the exercise by naming people we knew who we believed would make good magistrates, we were all able to identify 'suitable' people, but found it much more difficult to describe the qualities these people possessed which had caused us to choose them for the Bench. We should add that we had chosen people whom we had known well for some time. How much more difficult is the task of the Lord Chancellor's advisers who, as we have seen, are for the most part obliged to assess complete strangers and who base their decisions often on limited written information together with the candidates' performance in interview.

Our interest was, of course, not so much in the evolution of general criteria for assessment, but in how the selection committees applied these criteria to black candidates. We must emphasise first of all that almost all the A.C. and S.C. representatives we spoke to told us how anxious they were to recruit more black people to the Bench. Several of them told us that so anxious were they to appoint suitable black people that they were prepared, where necessary, to prefer a moderately good black candidate to an outstanding white one. The problem, we were told repeatedly, was a lack of 'suitable' black people putting themselves forward as candidates. The one thing that selection committees were not prepared to do was to accept someone whom they believed to be 'below standard'. As the secretary of one A.C., whose courts were 150 below the recommended establishment, told us, 'There's no point in lowering the standard just to get more people. The best way to ruin the standard of the lay magistracy . . . is to have people who are not as competent as they might be.'

When it came to the actual criteria for suitability, certain words and phrases were always cropping up, such as 'a balanced mind', 'common sense', 'a balanced attitude towards the police', 'the judicial mind', and 'a balanced personality'. As we have already mentioned (see pp.60-1) several Asian candidates, we were informed, fell at this particular hurdle, 'because of their different attitude towards justice', which was characterised by the chairman of Harley A.C. as not being able to see things from 'a judicial point of view. It's the injustice that they always look to'. When we questioned him further on this point, he explained that Asian candidates would tend to assess what was just or unjust in a particular situation rather than 'applying the law as it was written'.

A rather different generalisation about Asians was that they were too conformist. 'The Asian person is much more conforming and accepting of authority than the West Indian'. (Secretary, Metropole A.C.) One example we were given involved the supposed Asian attitude towards the police.

> There is perhaps a different attitude to authority and the police. If they [Asian candidates] are asked the question: 'You're sitting in judgement and the defendant says, "I didn't," and the police officer says, "You did",' there is sometimes a feeling outside this country that if the man in uniform says 'You did', then everyone should believe the man in uniform. (Chairman, Metropole S.C.)

Another complaint from the same source was that Asians lacked 'the committee mentality'. When asked what their attitude would be if they did not agree with the chairman of the bench in a particular case, Asians, we were told, would tend to say, 'I will listen to the more learned and respected person . . . If the chairman says I'm wrong, then I'll respect his opinion'. Such submissiveness, in the view of this and the other Metropole S.C. chairmen we interviewed, rendered such candidates unacceptable for the magistracy.

This 'failure to understand the way things work', to adapt to the 'English way of life' and to internalise its values was, we were told, a particularly significant factor in the Metropole A.C.'s assessment of black candidates.

> The number who get turned down from the comparatively few applicants from the Asian, West Indian and African communities is so often because *they have not embraced England*. (Secretary, A.C. [our emphasis])

> Many people who've not been brought up in this country, particularly people who find difficulty with the language, don't really understand how society works, even the courts, how they work. This is an added difficulty with ethnic minorities . . . a

good number of the candidates that we've had and not been able to appoint . . . have been coloured. It's because they didn't honestly understand how the country ticks. (Chairman, Metropole S.C.)

Yet it was not simply a matter of lacking familiarity with and understanding of the British way of life. It was also, we were informed, a question of 'the way they thought'. According to the reply we received from one A.C. to our questionnaire, adult West Indians, Africans or Asians, because of their backgrounds and way of life find it difficult to think in an 'English' way. This was echoed by the secretary of Metropole A.C. who told us: 'Potential magistrates have got to embrace some of the thinking of the community at large, for this thinking lies behind the laws laid down by Parliament.'

One way used by his committee to assess a black candidate's level of assimilation was to look at the organisations to which he or she belonged. For this purpose there were two distinct types of organisation, those which served only the interests of its members or a section of society and those concerned with the whole community. Thus, as we have mentioned, two of the Community Relations Councils in the area were seen as unlikely sources for prospective magistrates as they supposedly did not serve the community as a whole (see p.42). Political parties ('groups of different people with similar views') and Women's Institutes ('broadly based'), on the one hand were seen as serving the whole community, while immigrant organisations, on the other, had as their objectives, according to this secretary, 'the furtherance of the interests of their members rather than the furtherance of the interests of the community at large.' For this reason, not only did the committee consider unsuitable candidates whose only experience of public life had been within such immigrant organisations, but, as we have seen, they also omitted these organisations from the list of local groups invited to submit nominations for the magistracy (see p.42).

In the hands of the Metropole Advisory Committee, therefore, the concept of suitability had been extended far beyond questions of character, personal judgement and integrity, to include a qualifying test of participation in those groups and activities which the committee saw as furthering the interests of the whole community. We should add that we did not encounter such a clear distinction between community and sectional organisations elsewhere in the course of our research. However, the idea that magistrates should not be people who are confined within their own narrow social group or ethnic minority was prevalent in all the areas we visited, and in many of the replies to our questionnaires.

Extremism and controversy

Since the selectors often have to make decisions based entirely on the candidate's application form, interview performance and information about their community activities, it is perhaps not surprising that committees have tended to develop certain assumptions about the relationship between a person's public behaviour and his or her ability to judge others fairly. This is particularly in evidence in the way in which political views are assumed to provide some indication of a candidate's suitability. Any candidate, for example, who engages or has in the past engaged in what the committee regards as extremist political activities is immediately suspect. However, it was repeatedly emphasised by the A.C. and S.C. representatives to whom we spoke that it was not the candidates' politics which disqualified them from the Bench, but the failings which accompanied such political beliefs.

> You're not disqualifying the extreme left or the extreme right. What you're disqualifying are those who lack the ability to judge. (Secretary, Meadowport A.C.)

> . . . the fact that they will not enforce a law properly which does not accord with their views. (Secretary, Harley A.C.)

> . . . invariably impose a very harsh or very lenient policy for political rather than judicial reasons, in other words, could not distinguish one person from another or judge fairly someone with a different social background from himself. (Secretary, Harley A.C.)

One A.C. secretary who answered our questionnaire specifically related extremist views to racial groups when he told us that the committee often gets 'very unsuitable' Asian candidates, 'extremists both of the left and the right'.

More significant, however, from the point of view of ethnic minorities was the rejection as magistrates and the exclusion from the recruitment process of those individuals and groups that the committees considered 'controversial'. 'Controversial', as far as we were able to ascertain, meant engaging in activities of which the selectors disapproved and which attracted press or media attention. These activities included marches, demonstrations, picketing and public meetings. According to the secretary of one A.C., therefore, 'people prominent in the Grunwick dispute or the Southall race marches might not be identified as the most suitable candidates' while another secretary told us how they received applications from Asians who were 'people who go on demonstrations and cross swords with the police and are dead set against the establishment'. This according to the secretary was 'not the way to go about it'. The Metropole secretary also led us to believe that candidates proposed by organisations, such as Community Relations Councils, which had been prominent in such controversies were also unlikely to be warmly received by the A.C.

It was made plain to us that the reason that 'controversial' people were likely to be rejected had more to do with their lack of 'acceptability' than with their personal qualities. The Metropole committee felt that some people appearing in court might not feel confident that they would receive an unbiased judgement from such publicly known individuals and that this in time would undermine public confidence in the magistracy as a whole. Yet no evidence was offered in support of this argument and, as far as we were able to ascertain, no complaints on this score had been received either by the Lord Chancellor's Department or by local Advisory Committees. Moreover, from our experience of local newspaper reporting, we know that it was extremely rare, if not unknown, for the backgrounds of individual magistrates to be discussed in reports of court cases.[29]

Perhaps this attitude of the selectors as to who was and who was not 'suitable' to be a magistrate was best summed up by the secretary to the Branston A.C. who told us that his acid test of acceptability was, 'Would you be prepared to sit with that particular person as a colleague on the Bench?'

Recognition and respect by 'the community'

If A.C.s were to take literally the quotation from Lord Jowitt used by the Government in its booklet on the selection of J.P.s (and set out at the start of this Chapter) no one could be recommended to the Lord Chancellor for appointment until extensive enquiries had been carried out among his or her friends, neighbours and work-fellows. As we have seen, however, this is rarely possible and, although the extent and nature of investigations varies considerably from area to area and from candidate to candidate, it is true to say that in general the selectors tend to rely on references, information picked up from committee members or existing J.P.s and public knowledge, such as press reports, for their pre-interview assessment of a candidate's suitability.

It is also true, therefore, that less is known about the reputation of those candidates who do not move in the same social, political or voluntary work circles as existing members of the Bench. This would include many working-class candidates and members of ethnic minorities. It was never made very clear to us how the selection committees could realistically be expected to set about discovering whether these candidates were recognised as 'personally suitable' by those among whom they lived and worked.

Where this aspect of 'suitability' was treated seriously by A.C.s and S.C.s it tended, therefore, to be in a negative way. Sometimes it would reach the ears of the secretary or a member of the committee that this or that candidate was known for his dishonest business conduct, tendency to get into fights or marital infidelities. As a result the candidate would be disqualified. However, there appeared to be no clear or consistent criteria which could be applied to determine whether a candidate was or was not highly regarded or respected within his or her community. The only firm disqualifications for immediate appointment which we were able to identify were criminal convictions and recent divorce.

A person with criminal convictions, including motoring offences, was generally considered unsuitable for immediate appointment, because of their tarnished status within the community and the effect their appointment would have upon the confidence of that community in the magistracy. Where the offence was a minor matter, such as speeding, and the committee considered that the candidate was otherwise suitable in every way, the practice was often to 'let the Lord Chancellor decide'. According to an official within the Lord Chancellor's Office, their response was usually to delay appointment for a year or two. This, he informed us, had the dual purpose of allowing any publicity over the offence to die down and of letting the candidate know that this kind of behaviour was simply not acceptable in a J.P.

A similar policy seems to apply to people whose marriages have recently broken down. A member of the Thorburn A.C. told us that: '. . . because they [the magistrates] have to officiate in matrimonial [cases] . . . initially divorce is considered a disqualifying factor, but it is acceptable after three to five years . . .' In fact, only those magistrates appointed to the domestic panel have to sit on matrimonial cases, so that this argument for not appointing divorcees is not really persuasive. Possibly the real reason for postponing their appointment has more to do with the loss of social status that is supposedly involved in marriage breakdown.

Since it was not really possible in most cases to discover what 'the

70

community' felt either about a particular candidate or generally about divorce or people who had transgressed the speeding laws, there was a serious danger, in our view, that the notion of community recognition and respect could be used to impose the particular prejudices of the selection committee members or the Lord Chancellor and his officials. The idea of disqualifying people whose marriage had recently broken down, for example, seemed to us to be wholly unjustified in terms of the suitability of such people to do justice.

Unfortunately, the secrecy surrounding the selection process prevented us from investigating the impact of these policies on individual black candidates. We did, however, discover that at Branston, according to the A.C. secretary, the committee had despaired of finding an Asian candidate who was 'approved by all sides' of the Asian Community, and had ended up by appointing 'someone who is not actually involved in the community'. Our fear that this principle might be particularly prejudicial for Asian candidates was reinforced when we found that at Harley an Asian member of the A.C. was being used as a sort of hatchet man to decide who was and who was not 'acceptable to the Asian community'. The secretary of the Harley A.C. informed us that this Asian representative would say of a candidate, 'Nice chap, but he would not be acceptable to his colleagues'. This, according to the secretary, 'seems to happen to about three-quarters of the Asian candidates'.

Chapter 9

TIME

The minimum number of 'sittings', that is half-days in court, officially required of J.P.s each year is twenty-six. However, this figure gives a false impression of the actual demands made on the time of the majority of magistrates. Quite apart from their out-of-court duties, such as signing documents, attending meetings, giving talks, visiting institutions etc., the average number of sittings in our local study areas is far above the minimum requirement, as Table 5 indicates.

Table 5: Average Number of Sittings

Branston	54
Harley	44.5
Meadowport	50
Metropole County	47 (average for area's petty sessional divisions)
Thorburn	35

In practice, therefore, magistrates in these areas might well be asked to devote between thirty-five and fifty-four sittings a year to their duties on the local Bench. In addition, magistrates with two years or more experience are liable to be asked to sit with a judge in the Crown Court to hear appeals from magistrates' courts. Taking all these obligations into consideration, the hours of service of many J.P.s would be approaching twice the minimum laid down by the Lord Chancellor.

The pattern of attendances expected of individual magistrates depends upon the rota arrangements in their particular petty sessional division (P.S.D.). Most P.S.D.s in our local study expected J.P.s to sit on the same day every week or every other week. Meadowport, however, expected J.P.s to sit for a full week every quarter of a year. Moreover, all eligible J.P.s were expected to do Crown Court duty for a week a year and thus most Meadowport J.P.s have to be able to be available for five full weeks per annum. When we extended our enquiries beyond the areas covered by the local studies we found that the attendance expectation of J.P.s in most urban areas was generally well above the minimum. Table 6 sets out the replies received from the fifty-seven P.S.D.s who answered our questionnaire enquiry about the average number of sittings required in their area.

Table 6: Average Number of Sittings per Annum of Petty Sessional Divisions

Average number of sittings	20-24	25-29	30-34	34-39	40-44	45-49	50-54	Over 54
No. of P.S.D.s	4	1	4	13	16	10	6	3

The majority of A.C.s thus expected an average of between thirty-five and fifty court sessions from their J.P.s. The only places where the Lord Chancellor's minimum applied were in fact four small Benches in Lancashire. At the other end of the scale the average requirement at another Lancashire Bench was over sixty sessions a year.

Although a detailed examination of the reasons behind the high number of attendances expected by most courts was outside the scope of our study, it is worth recording that during the course of our interviews some A.C. and S.C. representatives pointed out that it was not simply a question of the rise in the volume of criminal work. In two cases they told us that a sizable minority of J.P.s were actually very keen to serve well over the minimum number of sessions on the Bench. In fact, they were so interested in the work that they opposed attempts to bring the number of magistrates up to the establishment recommended by the Lord Chancellor's Department for their area.[30] It seemed, therefore, that the fact that all the Commission areas in our local studies operated below, and three considerably below, the recommended establishment figure, might not have been entirely a result of a shortage of suitable applicants,[31] but also of a reluctance by the Bench itself to increase its number and so reduce the number of sessions each magistrate would be expected to attend.

We mention this because it gives some indication of the way in which the body of magistrates in particular areas could have a direct influence on the selection process. In areas where the number of magistrates was below that of the establishment figure the annual number of court sessions which candidates would be expected to attend, if appointed, would tend to be the average figure for that Bench. In some areas a candidate who could afford the time to attend only a maximum of twenty-six to thirty sessions a year could well be unacceptable since this would be out-of-step with the magistrates sitting on that Bench. According to several of the selectors we interviewed, finding suitable people who were willing to sit even the minimum of twenty-six sessions was becoming a serious problem.

What we are finding at the moment with high unemployment is that the people who are in work are working harder than ever before. In other words, we're finding that the businessman, the labourer, the schoolteacher, are very reluctant to give up the time, first of all because of all the staff shortages and, secondly, because, of course, they're frightened that come the next redundancy, they could be on it.' (Representative A.C., Harley)

These pressures were considered by many A.C. representatives as a major reason why so few black people put themselves forward or agreed to be nominated. One identified Asian shopkeepers as the sort of people who might make suitable magistrates were it not for the fact that their work effectively prevented them from finding the time necessary to make themselves available for the Bench. A number of selectors also pointed to the inability to take time off work coupled with the low rate of loss-of-earnings allowance offered to lay magistrates (now standing at £21 for over four hours and £10.50 for under four hours[32]) as the reasons why so few black people came forward. Although these reasons were reiterated by representatives of black organisations, as we shall see, there were other, possibly more important reasons. It is, therefore, impossible to predict whether a small reduction in the number of required sessions would make any real difference to the number or quality of black candidates. Yet what we can say with some confidence is that the sort of requirement which operates at Meadowport, whereby magistrates have to be available morning or afternoon for one whole week every quarter, or an average of sixty-plus sittings a year, may operate as an effective deterrent to potential black candidates whose work makes heavy demands on their time or whose employers are not prepared to give them time off.

The law relating to time off work for public duties is contained in Section 29 of the Employment Protection (Consolidation) Act 1978. Far from providing an absolute right to employees, the Act states that,

the amount of time off which an employee may be permitted to take . . . and the occasions on which . . . time off may be so taken are *those that may be reasonable in all the circumstances*, having regard particularly to the following:

(a) how much time off is required for the performance of the duties of the office . . . or as a member of the body in question, and how much time off is required for the performance of the particular duty;

(b) how much time off the employee has already been

permitted under this section or [in relation to trade union duties and activities];

(c) the circumstances of the employer's business and the effect of the employee's absence on the running of the business.

The employees remedy if the employer refuses to allow him or her to take time off work to sit on the Bench is to complain to an industrial tribunal, which may make an award of compensation. If the employee is dismissed for taking time off, it is extremely unlikely that the tribunal would order reinstatement, although there have been no reported cases on this issue.

In our interviews of black magistrates and black community representatives the problem of taking time off work was frequently raised in response to questions as to why so few black people put themselves forward for the magistracy. The chairman of one Asian organisation told us, for example, 'Most Asians are employed in manual jobs in which it would be difficult to obtain time off.'

The link between type of employment and the possibility of becoming a magistrate was seen by some as favouring people in particular types of employment and precluding from the magistracy those who were most likely to be representative of a large part of the black community. 'You need to have some sort of cushy job because of the times the courts sit. Therefore there is very little chance of attracting the sort of people I would like to see as magistrates.' (Chairman, Afro-Caribbean organisation, Metropole County)

Several of the people we interviewed went on to suggest that the pressure caused by the high level of unemployment had made matters worse, because to request time off in the current labour situation meant 'putting one's job at risk'. 'A lot of people would want their names to go forward, but would say, "I'm scared to ask for the day off".' (Executive member, Afro-Caribbean organisation, Branston)

In a more general way the well-documented discrimination against black people in the labour market[33] has had the effect of creating a high level of anxiety, not only about the possibility of losing one's job, but also in relation to promotion and career prospects. One Asian J.P. in Metropole County was convinced that the time he took off from the school where he taught has severely affected his chances of further promotion. Another teacher told us how she felt when she was approached to allow her name to go forward for selection:

I was a more junior teacher and I was in schools where there were other teachers . . . there before me who were J.P.s. I knew how people looked at them when they went out one day a week. That's one of the reasons I didn't [let my name go forward]. I wanted promotion in my work and I wasn't going to let being a J.P. prevent me from making my way up the ladder in my main job, and that was the main reason for not letting my name go forward. (Chairperson, Afro-Caribbean organisation)

For those who had no job the prospect of sitting on the Bench was even less inviting, for they believed that being a J.P. could well reduce their chances of finding employment. Some confirmation of this fear was given to us by the senior officer of a well-established Asian organisation. He told us that, though employees of the organisation were contractually allowed time off for magistrates' duties, the organisation had had 'bad experiences' with someone who took one-and-a-half days off work. As a result they will no longer employ anyone who is a J.P.. Brian Cooke, the present Secretary of Commissions, drew attention in a recent article to the way the employment situation is affecting the lay magistracy. He wrote that, 'a disturbing feature was the number of magistrates [who] have found it necessary to resign from the commission on account of their employment or because it may jeopardise their chances of new employment or retention of their present employment.' (Cooke, 1984, p.71)

Chapter 10

BALANCE

It is in the public interest that persons of every social grade should be appointed Justices of the Peace and that working men with a first-hand knowledge of the conditions of life among their own class should be appointed . . . (Royal Commission on the Selection of Justices of the Peace, 1910, p.15)

In the context of the long history of Justices of the Peace, the idea that magistrates' Benches should be 'balanced' is a very recent innovation. It was less than eighty years ago that the qualification of property ownership for appointment to the Bench was finally abolished and only sixty-four years ago that women first became eligible for appointment. Today, however, all those concerned in the selection process talk freely of their efforts to balance the Bench in terms of politics, occupation and gender as if balancing is an attempt to create in each area a body of magistrates which reflects proportionally the local population.

Our research, however, found little evidence to support this idealised notion of balance. Instead, it appeared to us that balancing was rather a legacy of the pressure which the Liberal and later the Labour Party brought to bear on the Lord Chancellor to end the near monopoly which the Tories held over the lay magistracy. The effect of this legacy has been to make the Lord Chancellor and A.C.s aware of the importance of giving the magistracy an acceptable face to avoid the criticism that the Bench is dominated by any one political group or faction of the community. One A.C. recently published an article to encourage nominations for the Bench, which stated: 'The question of balance is of vital importance if the glib criticism that all magistrates are middle-aged and middle-class is to be totally answered.'

Yet, in the course of our research we found that these two very different objectives, making the Bench representative and giving it a politically acceptable appearance, were repeatedly being equated by A.C.s. However, this confusion was fostered and encouraged by the Lord Chancellor's Department. Sir Thomas Skyrme, the recently retired Secretary of Commissions, responsible for the selection process writes, for example:

The declared policy of each Lord Chancellor since 1945 has been to make sure that *each Bench is a microcosm of the local community and this amounts to seeing that in every petty sessional division there are at least some justices from each of the principal social and political groups in the area and that the Bench is not dominated by any one group.* (1979, pp.62-3) (our emphasis)

It is our view that giving the Bench an acceptable appearance is a far cry from the idea of creating in the magistracy a 'microcosm of the local community' and attempts to equate these aims can be highly misleading.

The truth is that the suitability criteria together with the demands made of J.P.s in terms of time and financial sacrifice favour, as we have seen, the professions and articulate, committee-minded people who are active in political, voluntary or charitable organisations. These people tend to be white, middle-class and usually vote Conservative,[34] so that balancing the Bench has in the main become a struggle to prevent the Bench being dominated by such groups.[35] The need 'to balance the Bench' has, therefore, to a large extent been created by past conflict between the policy of the Lord Chancellor's Department and the approach of A.C.s towards their task, which strongly favour particular social groups with particular attitudes and experience.

Moreover, since the selectors maintain that those people chosen as magistrates are so fair and just that they would never allow their decisions to be affected by prejudices derived from class background, ideological beliefs or experiences, A.C.s do not see themselves bound to ensure that the Bench represents a cross-section of attitudes and opinions on those issues which are the daily fare of magistrates courts.

The only direct attempt to achieve a spread of opinions on the Bench concerns the political affiliation of magistrates. However, there is little relationship between political views and attitudes towards crime and justice. It is true that 'the left' has traditionally been associated with a liberal approach towards punishment, and 'the right' with a more retributive, deterrent attitude. However, it is by no means unusual to find, for example, trade union leaders from working-class backgrounds with extremely disciplinarian views on punishment, and Conservatives with interventionist and liberal beliefs about crime and the way to control it.

There is no attempt to balance the Bench in terms of the views held by J.P.s towards police powers, crime-control methods, the use of prison, probation and social-work intervention, etc.. The selectors allow themselves complete discretion in their choice of social and political groups for balancing purposes and in the way the balancing exercise is undertaken; and we found that they tended to ignore certain important social groups in the balancing process. These included not only people whom the selectors considered to be 'extremists', but also the under-thirties, single parents and the unemployed. In some areas religion is recognised as a balancing factor, but in others it is ignored.

The usually acceptable social divisions have been political affiliation, sex, age, social background and occupation. Yet the fact that these divisions are not mutually exclusive provides scope for yet further exercise of discretion by the selectors. A male Conservative factory-worker, for example, could in theory be regarded for balancing purposes as a male, a wage-earner or a Tory. In practice this issue would almost certainly be resolved by his appointment as a wage-earner, even if this meant increasing the already high level of male Tories on the Bench, since suitable wage-earners are reputedly so difficult to find. Conversely, a socialist female teacher could well find herself rejected or having her appointment deferred, because she is a member of the teaching profession, and any professional or occupational group is seen by the Lord Chancellor as being over-represented if it exceeds 15 per cent of the Bench. Yet, we found that the assumptions behind these categories and their interpretation were never challenged or even adequately analysed by those responsible for the selection and appointment of J.P.s. We can understand why it may be objectionable for a Bench to be totally dominated by one profession, but it was never made at all clear to us why a female socialist comprehensive-school teacher should be treated for balancing purposes in the same category as a male SDP college lecturer.

A recent innovation made by certain A.C.s has been the introduction of the idea of geographical spread. The purpose of this is to prevent a concentration of magistrates from one or more districts within the commission catchment area. Thus one A.C. turned down two out of three otherwise suitable middle-class women, because all three happened to live in the same street. As a positive measure, the aim of the policy of geographical spread is to make the Bench representative of all parts of the commission area, town and country, suburb and inner city. However as a practical proposition it does not provide any advance on the existing balancing factors, for, as with these factors, it is introduced only after the suitability criteria have ruled out many candidates. Moreover, from the point of view of the administration of justice, differences in magistrates' addresses are no more likely to correspond in any systematic way to different attitudes towards crime, police powers, punishment, etc., than are differences in political affiliation. As far as black candidates are concerned, the introduction of geographical spread by some A.C.s does not on its own appear to have resulted in any significant increase in the number of black magistrates appointed to the Bench. In any event, race has since 1961 been accepted as a legitimate balancing factor by the Lord Chancellor's Department (Skyrme, p. 62) (although no records are kept on the racial backgrounds of appointees), so A.C.s which took this factor seriously would already be on the look-out for suitable black J.P.s.

How then was race used as a balancing factor by A.C.s? As we have emphasised already, what emerged from our interview with selectors was a consistent assurance of the importance of finding more suitable black J.P.s. This, we were told, by the representatives of several A.C.s, outweighed all other balancing considerations. Thus, a black 'suitable' Tory university lecturer would almost certainly be appointed even though the Bench concerned might be overloaded with Tories and members of the teaching profession.

Although there was some variation between selection committees, the only distinction that was usually made for balancing purposes was between candidates of Asian and those of Afro-Caribbean (including African) origin. The Secretary of Harley A.C. told us, for example, that the committee did not attempt to distinguish between Indians and Pakistanis, although he personally recognised that there were considerable religious and cultural differences between the two groups. This policy contributed to the fact that the local, mainly Moslem, Pakistani community had comparatively few representatives on the Bench in relation to their numbers in the population. This provoked a bitter complaint from a prominent member of the Pakistani community. Interviewer: 'Did you know there were only three Moslems on the Bench?'[36] Interviewee: 'Three Moslem representatives out of 50,000 people — to me it's less than token. I'd use the word "preposterous". I think it's absolutely unacceptable.'

Although we formed the impression that Harley A.C. wished to increase the number of Moslem J.P.s, there was no clear commitment to applying considerations of balance. Indeed, the chairman of the committee informed us in no uncertain terms that while he saw the need for some black magistrates, he refused to break it down between black and white and between Moslem and Hindu and between Asians and Afro-Caribbeans. 'It's men and women and their backgrounds.'

An important issue which we identified in relation to racial balance is that of representation. The principle that magistrates should serve the *whole community* and not just a sector of the community is currently being interpreted by the Lord Chancellor's

Department and by almost all the A.C.s with which we had contact as disqualifying any candidates who in interview state that they see themselves as *representing* a political party, group, organisation or sector of the community. 'I don't believe in taking *representatives*' (our emphasis) the chairman of Harley A.C. told us firmly. While the chairman of one of the Metropole S.C.s spoke of 'a rush of candidates from a women's organisation who saw themselves as *representatives*' and were therefore denied approval. So, while black candidates may be acceptable because they are a member of a social group which is inadequately reflected in the make-up of the Bench, they will be rejected if they see themselves as *representatives* of that group.

After listening to several such comments we formed the impression that there was considerable confusion among selectors as to the meaning of 'representative' and that in interview this confusion may have been passed on to candidates with the result that they were rejected wholly or partly on the basis of a false impression they may have given in response to ambiguous questions. The word 'representative' can be used in the sense of being a delegate, for example someone who, to quote one A.C. secretary, insists on 'putting forward the employer's view or the trade union's view' and, who, presumably, perceives him or herself as accountable to the particular political party or other sponsoring organisation when considering the line he or she should take on judicial issues such as sentencing, licensing, juvenile crime, etc.. It is, in our view, quite correct for A.C.s to refuse to accept candidates on this basis, since to appoint them might result in court decisions being influenced by direct external pressure. We do not accept, however, that black communities, as such, have coherent, consensual policies on these issues. It is, therefore, nonsense to talk of candidates representing the black community on the Bench. Black candidates may identify broadly with the hopes, fears and aspirations of many black people just as some white people will identify with certain class or political values and attitudes. There is, however, no reason to think that they will use their position on the Bench to promote, for example, 'Pakistani policies' or take their orders as to how they should, for example, sentence burglars from the leaders of the local black communities. And unless there is strong evidence that they belong to a group with clear policies on the sorts of issues which come before magistrates' courts and that they would allow their allegiance to override their judgement as J.P.s they should not be rejected.

From what we were told by those responsible for selecting magistrates, it appears that many committees took the view that black candidates merely had to suggest, in reply to interview questions, that they regarded themselves as 'representatives of their community' and that would be an end of their chances of selection. Usually, it seems that no attempt was made to explain precisely what was meant by the word or what effect, if any, the candidates' representative capacity would have on their ability to do justice. In other words, the key word 'representative' appears to have been used, perhaps unwittingly, by committees in a misleading way, drawing them to make a false distinction between candidates who would in their decision-making follow their personal beliefs and values — beliefs and values which others from the same racial background might indeed share — and those candidates who would use their position on the Bench to promote the policies of the pressure group or political party to which they belonged.

The issue of representation had clearly caused problems in the past for selectors faced with Pakistani candidates. For among the documents which the Lord Chancellor's Department issues to all A.C.s (see Appendix V) was a specimen questionnaire, originating from an unnamed A.C., which contained the following questions:

Supplementary questions asked to a Pakistani immigrant candidate

(a) Would you regard yourself if you became a magistrate as in some way representing the Pakistani community?

(b) Do you think that, if you became a magistrate, members of the Pakistani community would regard you as in some respect representing them on the Bench? Would their attitude put you under any pressure and how would you cope with it?

Our suggestion that the inclusion of these questions might be interpreted as discrimination against Pakistani candidates was firmly rejected by an official of the Lord Chancellor's Department. He maintained that it was chance that Pakistanis were singled out for attention and that the question could equally be asked of any other candidate. He mentioned, however, that the A.C. from which the questionnaire originated may have been experiencing particular problems with candidates from the Pakistani community. Whatever the reason for its inclusion as a specimen question for the use of A.C.s, we do not find that these questions clarify the ambiguities involved in the use of the term 'representative'. If anything, they make it more obscure since, while the second question raises the issue of delegation, it fails to specify what is meant by *'representing a community on the Bench'* or the sort of attitudes which might put a magistrate *'under pressure'*. Unless these matters are defined in the questions asked, we would anticipate that many candidates would have difficulty in understanding what the committee was referring to. While we sympathise with those selectors who wish to exclude from the Bench anyone who looks to an organisation, group, party, etc., outside the magistracy for guidance or instructions on how they should exercise their judgement in court, we feel that the broad notion of 'being a representative' is far too wide an exclusionary condition.

One could well have people who see themselves as 'representatives' of a particular party, group, organisation or community in the sense that they identify with that body, but who nevertheless would make model magistrates in that they would not consciously allow their decisions to be influenced by their affiliations. Conversely, there may be those who do not see themselves as belonging to any such body, but who may permit their judgement to be distorted by strong personal beliefs. These beliefs may or may not be similar or identical to the values of some external body. Whether or not a person calls himself or herself 'a representative', therefore, may be quite irrelevant to his or her ability to do justice in court.

Moreover, there can be absolutely no justification for the discriminatory manner in which this requirement is applied in practice. Asking Pakistani candidates if they saw themselves as representatives of their community would only fall short of racial discrimination if all candidates, of whatever racial background, were asked about all the possible affiliations and sympathies which might influence their decision-making. White candidates would therefore have to convince selectors that their religious or ethnic group and their affiliations to clubs, organisations, political parties, etc., would not affect their judgement in court.

We would suggest that the selectors' object of excluding people from the Bench whose independence might be suspect could be achieved by other, non-discriminatory methods, such as presenting all candidates with hypothetical cases designed to test their independence of judgement. We fully accept that candidates who set out to deceive the selectors are unlikely to be caught out by such methods, but they are even less likely to reveal their true colours by being asked whether or not they see themselves as representatives. The only effective way to exclude such people from the Bench is to monitor their performance in actual courtroom cases.

Pakistani candidates interviewed by the Harley A.C. find themselves doubly in difficulty. Not only do they have to show in order to be selected that they would not 'represent' any particular section of the Pakistani community on the Bench — a difficult task in itself, because the A.C., according to the secretary, has 'noticed that they have a tremendous loyalty to their own political party'. But they also have to demonstrate that they are acceptable to (without being a 'representative' of) the Pakistani community as a whole; and, according to the same secretary 'almost any person that is put forward is unacceptable in a very extreme way to three-quarters of their own community'.

The selectors at Harley seem to have moved a long way from the idea that their role is simply to select candidates who are suitable people to administer justice. Their present efforts to balance the Bench and avoid candidates who see themselves as representatives could well discriminate against Asian people.

The 'Failure' Rate among Black Candidates

While it was exceptional for A.C.s and S.C.s to adopt the improvement of racial balance as a formal policy, it was by no means unusual for them to 'keep a look out' for likely black candidates with the intention of improving the representation of Afro-Caribbeans and Asians on the Bench. Moreover, it was highly unlikely that considerations of balance would lead to the exclusion of black candidates who would otherwise have been considered 'suitable'.

One matter we have not yet discussed is the frequency with which black candidates were rejected as 'unsuitable' in comparison with other candidates. We obtained information from fifteen A.C.s and S.C.s on the number of black and other candidates who were recommended to the Lord Chancellor between 1980 and 1982. Overall, we found the failure rate for black candidates to be slightly higher than for other candidates, as Table 6 indicates. Afro-Caribbean candidates, with a failure rate of 70 per cent fared marginally better than Asians whose failure rate was 78.2 per cent. It is important to note, however, that the figure for Asians is somewhat influenced by the decisions of two A.C.s and one S.C. who between them accounted for forty-two out of the total of 101 Asian applicants. Of these forty-two, only seven were recommended, a failure rate of 83.4 per cent. Yet, even if one sets aside the decisions of these three committees, the failure rate for Asians was still 74.6 per cent, slightly higher than for Afro-Caribbeans and 'other' candidates.

A few candidates did not reach the recommendation stage, because, although 'approved' by the selection committee, they decided to withdraw before their names were passed on to the Lord Chancellor. Our figures for the failure rate include such candidates, because from the statistical evidence available to us it was impossible to distinguish between rejection and withdrawal. Our evidence in fact suggests that black candidates are no more likely to withdraw than white. When this question was put to A.C.s and S.C.s in our questionnaire, only one of the twenty-one who responded to this question stated that black candidates withdraw more frequently than others. This suggests that the vast majority of black candidates who fail to be recommended do not withdraw, but are rejected by selection committees.

Table 6: Recommendation and Failure Rates According to Racial Background of Candidate, 1980-82*

	Afro-Caribbean	Asian	Others	Total
Candidates	58	101	2307	2466
Recommended by A.C. or S.C.	17**	22	641	690
Failure rate %	70.1	78.2	72.2	72.4

*For one of the committees figures were available only for 1980-81.
**Five had received no applications from Afro-Caribbeans.

Finally, as we have already pointed out, it is extremely unusual for the Lord Chancellor to intervene once a candidate has been approved and recommended by an A.C.. However, we did come across cases where the role of the Lord Chancellor and his office was not simply that of a rubber stamp. Three A.C.s told us how they decided to defer recommending black candidates after 'consultation' with the Lord Chancellor's Department. The clearest examples of active intervention by the Lord Chancellor, however, concerned the A.C. reconsidering its recommendation in respect of two Asian candidates after the committee had been provided with 'new information' from officials in the Department together with a suggestion that this information be, to use the officials' phraseology, 'taken into consideration by the committee'. Neither candidate was appointed.

Chapter 11

RACIAL PREJUDICE AND DISCRIMINATION

> *Discrimination is not 'a series of isolated and distinguishable events', but a 'far more complex, pervasive and institutionalised phenomenon, explicable and remediable only by reference to systems and effects'.*
>
> *(U.S. Senate Report on Discrimination, 1971.)*

It was not the purpose of our research to track down and expose villains guilty of racial prejudice and discrimination. Our concern was to examine the attitudes of selection officials towards black people and the effect these attitudes might have — and were actually having — upon the operation of the appointments system, and on the number and characteristics of black magistrates. However, the attitudes themselves are important as they help to create a general background of shared beliefs and values against which decisions are taken. We consider it important, therefore, to comment on the way in which some of the officials we interviewed offered stereotypes of black people and generalised, for example, about 'Asians' and 'West Indians' from these stereotypes. We appreciate that some of those interviewed might not have expressed those views without being asked specific questions about black people. Nevertheless, we must express our deep concern, firstly at finding racial prejudice among selection committee members advising Ministers of State on whom they should appoint to judicial posts of some power and importance. And secondly, at the fact that not one of these officials seemed to have the slightest awareness that they were doing anything other than presenting a fair and accurate picture of black people. Let us now give some examples, some of which has already been pointed out earlier in this report.

'Pakistanis' were variously described to us by the secretaries, chairmen and members of selection committees as 'more nervous than others', either 'tending to give the impression that they are not expecting to succeed', or 'pompous' 'having a tremendous loyalty to their political party' and 'having rigorous views'. Indians, we were told 'answer questions in the way that the enquirer wants to be responded to', while Asians generally, according to one chairman, 'did not look at things from a judicial point of view', and, according to an A.C.secretary, were over-respectful towards authority and, in particular, to the police. 'West Indians', on the other hand, were supposedly less conforming than Asians. They were described by one A.C. secretary as 'volatile and excitable' and as 'slow speaking and having slow reactions' by another.

Our concern here is that these statements are gross generalisations based for the most part upon observations of a small number of Asians and Afro-Caribbeans in a limited range of situations. Yet some of the people who made these remarks were only too willing to reject white people as 'unsuitable' for the magistracy because they had shown themselves to be biased or incapable of forming a balanced view. Whether prejudice among the Lord Chancellor's advisors and those responsible for operating the selection system was translated into acts of direct discrimination against individual black candidates must be a matter of speculation on our part, as we were unable to gain access to the committees' and interview panels' deliberations. Certainly, we have no direct evidence that these officials ever rejected a candidate purely on the basis of his or her colour. Indeed, we have already accepted that most of those to whom we spoke saw themselves as eager to find more black members for the Bench. However, the issue of discrimination does not end with these examples of stereotyping.

In 1978 an unsuccessful woman candidate for the Bench took proceedings in an Industrial Tribunal against the Lord Chancellor on the grounds that he had discriminated against her and had therefore contravened the provisions of the Sex Discrimination Act.[37] Unfortunately, the Industrial Tribunal hearing the case, without examining the merits of the complaint, ruled that it did not have jurisdiction, so the action failed. On appeal, the Employment Appeal Tribunal, while upholding the decision of the Industrial Tribunal, left open the important question as to whether the appointment of magistrates is covered by the Sex Discrimination Act. The issue revolves around the fine legal point concerning who actually appoints magistrates. If the appointer is the Lord Chancellor then, as a minister of the Crown, he is bound by the Act not to do anything which infringes the Act's definition of sexual discrimination. If, on the other hand, appointments are made by the Crown itself, then the appointments system would be outside the jurisdiction of the Act.

This case is important for our purposes, because the Race Relations Act 1976 has almost the same wording as the Sex

Discrimination Act. If, therefore, magistrates, as seems likely, are appointed by the Lord Chancellor rather than by the Crown, Section 76 of the Race Relations Act would apply and the Lord Chancellor would be under a statutory duty to avoid discrimination as defined by Section 1 of this Act (see below). This statutory duty would extend both to the appointment itself and to the way in which A.C.s operate in selecting people and advising the Lord Chancellor. Yet in order to win in the courts an unsuccessful candidate would have not only to obtain a favourable ruling on the technical legal point, but also to overcome the secrecy barrier and the vague and general criteria for selection which leave so much to the discretion and interpretation of S.C.s. This would be a formidable task. Nevertheless we believe it to be a worthwhile exercise to examine the results of our research against the Race Relations Act's anti-discrimination provisions, not because we necessarily accept the rather narrow view of discrimination provided by the Act, but because they do at least offer some clear, public criteria by which to adjudge the existence of discrimination.

Section 1 of the Race Relations Act 1976 states as follows:

Racial Discrimination

A person discriminates against another in any circumstances relevant for the purposes of any provision of this Act if —

(a) on racial grounds he treats that other less favourably than he treats or would treat any other person; or

(b) he applies to that other a requirement or condition which he applies or would apply equally to persons not of the same racial group as that other but —

(i) which is such that the proportion of persons of the same racial group as that other who can comply with it is considerably smaller than the proportion not of that racial group who can comply with it; and

(ii) which he cannot show to be justifiable irrespective of the colour, race, nationality or ethnic or national origins of the person to whom it is applied; and

(iii) which is to the detriment of that other because he cannot comply with it.

Direct Discrimination

Instances of direct discrimination, that is less favourable treatment, occurred during the selection process within our local study areas. The first was at Metropole County, where the A.C. deliberately excluded black organisations and Community Relations Councils

(C.R.C.s) from its list of local bodies to be approached in its search for candidates for the Bench. It may be, of course, that some white organisations were also excluded because they were 'not interested in the community' but only in 'a certain branch of the community'. Yet this would not make the policy of the Metropole County A.C. any less discriminatory, as the C.R.C.s and black organisations in the area were clearly treated less favourably than other, predominantly white, organisations. The reason for this less favourable treatment was undoubtedly racial in nature, since the C.R.C.s and black organisations were perceived as 'serving the interests of black people' and not the community at large. The interests of black people were, therefore, seen as separate from the general welfare of the community.

The second example of direct discrimination concerns the requirement at Harley and Branston that Asian candidates should be 'acceptable to the whole Asian community' (see p.71). This we regard as direct discrimination since no similar requirement was imposed on other candidates in relation to 'their communities'. We have no doubt, for instance, that some local Tory politicians who sat on the Bench were regarded by some Labour supporters as anathemas and vice versa, but we are equally sure that the selection committees would not have rejected these politicians as magistrates simply because they were heartily disliked by members of the other party. Similarly, ideological divisions within political parties were not treated by the committees as relevant factors for selection purposes. We were, therefore, disturbed to learn that the Branston S.C. had 'despaired' of finding an Asian candidate who was 'approved by all sides of the Asian community' and had resorted to appointing someone who 'was not actually involved in the community'. We were even more disturbed by the account we received of the activities of the Asian member of the Harley A.C. who, as we have seen, effectively vetoed about three-quarters of Asian candidates, 'because they are not acceptable to [their] colleagues' in the Asian community.

Thirdly, it was clear to us from our interviews that for some A.C.s and S.C.s the fact that a candidate was from an ethnic minority was in itself a sufficient ground for additional questions to be asked about that candidate's 'loyalty' to the principles of justice and about possible conflicts between those principles and the pursuit of sectarian interests. Where this occurred, it could be held that there was direct discrimination because, in the case of white candidates, such questions were raised only when the candidate belonged to some specific group or organisation whose policies or interests were concerned with issues which were likely to be the subject of judicial decisions. Put more directly, if you are a

Pakistani or Caribbean candidate, you have to convince the committee that you do not intend to use your position on the Bench to serve your community. There is as we have seen an immediate assumption that the black population constitutes a clearly identifiable, integral community with interests and aspirations common to all or almost all its members. If you are a white candidate, however, you need not expect to be questioned on whether you see yourself as a representative of the white middle class or whether you intend to pursue class and racial policies when you sit on the Bench.

Indirect Discrimination

One instance of indirect discrimination concerns the language requirement and the way it was applied by the selectors. All the A.C.s and S.C.s in our local project insisted that candidates whose names went forward to the Lord Chancellor should have a sufficient command of English to enable them to carry out their duties on the Bench. There can be no doubt that this requirement is indirectly discriminatory against Asian candidates, since for a substantial proportion of Pakistanis and Indians living in this country English is not their first language. The Asian population is therefore less able than white people to comply with this requirement. Whether this requirement can be justified under Section (1)(b)(iii) is a matter which we shall discuss later. What concerns us at present is the way in which the linguistic ability of candidates was assessed.

To begin with, in the course of our research we came across no A.C. or S.C. who made any attempt to test linguistic skills in any systematic way. There were no formal tests of written or spoken English, such as comprehension or vocabulary exercises. Apart from Branston, where the S.C. secretary saw black candidates individually before they were chosen or rejected for interview, all the other A.C.s and S.C.s we studied used the candidate's answers to questions asked in formal interviews as the main and, in some cases, only basis for assessing his or her competence in English. As for the ability to read and understand written English quickly, an important skill for magistrates who often have to cope with reports and other documents during the course of their decision-making, some selectors, it seems, ask Asian candidates whether they are competent in written English or simply assume that this must be the case from the nature of the candidate's job (see pp.62-3). The candidate's completion of the application form could not be relied upon as evidence of his or her ability in written English, since this

90

could easily have been done by someone else or with the assistance of another person.

The other important point we wish to make about the requirement of English language competence is that the issue was likely to arise only in relation to Asian candidates or, very occasionally, to other candidates who spoke with a foreign accent. Provided a candidate performed adequately in the formal interview, it is probable that no questions would be raised about his or her competence to cope with written reports or the sort of complex issues which are sometimes presented through oral evidence in the courtroom. If committees are indeed applying a language competence requirement only to Asian candidates, then this constitutes *direct* discrimination.

The second 'requirement' which appeared to us to be discriminatory against black people was the rather vague notion which appeared in one form or another in the thinking of almost all the A.C. and S.C. representatives whom we met — that candidates should have sufficient knowledge of 'the English way of life'. It was expressed most forcibly by the secretary and chairman of Metropole A.C. who told us that candidates should 'think in an English way', 'embrace some of the thinking of the community', 'understand how the country ticks', and 'embrace England'. Once again, if this 'requirement' is applied only to black candidates, it is *direct* discrimination. Even if it is imposed on all candidates, it may well be *indirect* discrimination, for black people from overseas and many of those who live here might well be less likely than white people to possess the sort of knowledge that selectors consider to relate to 'the English way of life'. Moreover, as with the English language requirement, no attempt was made to test in any systematic way such matters as might be relevant to fulfilling this 'requirement', such as the candidate's knowledge of how British institutions operate.

Justification for Indirect Discrimination

In order for courts or tribunals to find indirect discrimination proven under the Race Relations Act they must be satisfied that the person imposing the discriminatory requirement or condition 'cannot show it to be justified irrespective of the colour, race, ethnic or national origins of the person to whom it is applied'. Sec. (1)(b)(iii). The white paper on which the statute was based makes the point that such justification must be 'substantially related to job performance'. In the case of magistrates' selection this leads to problems of interpretation for the only formal requirements and conditions are exclusionary categories laid down by the Lord Chancellor (see pp.28-9) and relate to such matters as the age of candidates and whether they hold offices or jobs incompatible with being a J.P. It is not these formal requirements which are discriminatory, but the vague and ill-defined criteria which the selectors impose in their search for people who are 'suitable' to sit on the Bench. However, as one legal commentator on race relations states, the statutory provisions covering discrimination would be ineffective if they related only to formal job qualifications. He writes:

> The absence of formal objective criteria does not mean that no standards at all govern employment decisions . . . applicants are generally asked about a host of related matters such as prior experience, work record, reasons for leaving previous employment and record of arrests and convictions. Since the employer must be satisfied on these points before the applicant will be hired, these 'personal' criteria function as requirements and conditions of employment. This wider interpretation accords with the policy of the Act to prohibit the use of standards that unintentionally but effectively disadvantage racial minorities. (Lustgarten, 1980, p.45)

We would argue, therefore, that, if the appointment of magistrates were within the jurisdiction of the Act, it would be valid for the courts to examine the vague criteria which different A.C.s and S.C.s use to determine whether a candidate is 'suitable'.

In considering whether a job requirement or condition is justified, courts and tribunals have to take into account all the circumstances in which they are imposed.[38] Moreover, it has been decided recently by the Court of Appeal that 'justifiable' imposes a lesser standard than 'necessary',[39] so that even if a requirement is not strictly necessary for the job, or the same control over the suitability of candidates could be achieved by other non-discriminatory means, the employer may still argue successfully that in all the circumstances the requirement is 'justifiable'. In relation to the selection of magistrates, therefore, the question that needs to be answered is this: Can the formal and informal criteria which are applied by selectors and which discriminate indirectly against black people be justified in all the circumstances?

Applying this test to the language competence requirement, we would certainly accept that a reasonable command of English is not only a justifiable, but an essential requirement for a magistrate. What we find discriminatory, however, is the way in which this requirement is interpreted and applied in the selection process. We believe that there may be considerable differences between candidates' ability to answer questions in formal interviews and their capacity for understanding the evidence and issues presented in a courtroom case, discussing these with other members of the bench and presenting reasoned arguments in defence of their decisions. While the interviewers may be able to make accurate assessments of language ability in respect of some candidates, they may be hopelessly inaccurate in respect of others who, through nerves or unfamiliarity with the situation, may do themselves less than justice. Moreover, as we have already pointed out (pp.62-3) the selectors make no attempt to assess the ability of either black or white candidates in comprehension of written English.

Furthermore, certain of the selectors to whom we spoke appeared to be applying discriminatory and unjustifiable criteria in their assessment of language ability when they said that they were looking for people with the potential to take on the role of court chairperson. Applying this standard to candidates would exclude all those who spoke falteringly or with a strong accent on the grounds that they would lack dignity and that there would be difficulty in understanding their courtroom pronouncements. It seems to us that the two roles of magistrate and chairperson are quite distinct and should remain so for the purposes of selecting J.P.s. Indeed, some areas run courses for chairpersons which seek to train J.P.s in the specific skills necessary for this role. It is quite possible for a magistrate to remain on the Bench without ever becoming a chairperson, so that a candidate's skills in speech making are largely irrelevant to his or her capacity to sit on the Bench. Furthermore some people might well develop 'chairperson's skills' some time after having been appointed as magistrates and all magistrates have to take a chairpersonship course before sitting as such.

The second point concerning the method of testing language skills places the selectors on even weaker ground, for there already exist job-related tests of competence in English such as that used by the Temporary Registration and Assessment Board for doctors. It would not be difficult to devise an objective test of comprehension and expression in oral English which could be applied to all candidates, black or white, for whom English was not their first language. In view of the concern expressed about the ability of candidates to read and assimilate rapidly the contents of written reports and other documents, we would suggest a further test specifically related to these skills which *all* candidates would be required to take. The continued use of interviews to test ability in English is, therefore, unjustifiable in all the circumstances and constitutes in our view indirect discrimination.

The requirements of 'knowledge of the English way of life' raises greater problems. For a start, it is difficult to assess the merits of the requirement in terms of its job-relatedness without having some idea of what is meant by 'the English way of life'. However, the vagueness of this phrase did not prevent an Industrial Tribunal in 1978 from accepting the decision of the Council of Legal Education that 'all barristers must have a knowledge of the English way of life'.[40] Despite this Tribunal's willingness to uphold the validity of this general requirement, we find it unacceptable in the case of magistrates. Firstly, we wonder what particular aspects of the 'English way of life' would be considered essential knowledge for those appointed to the Bench. Would a general knowledge of British institutions and traditions be sufficient or would magistrates also have to know something about the sort of lives led by all those who appear in court before them? One wonders, for example, how many existing magistrates have seen the inside of a Social Security office or stood on the terraces at a football match. Secondly, there is a serious danger of 'the English way of life' becoming equated in the minds of the selectors with 'the white way of life'. This ignores the fact that most Asians and Afro-Caribbeans living in this country have as much right to call themselves 'English' as most white people who live here. They also have the right to expect that those who pass judgement upon them should have some knowledge of *their* way of life. For these reasons, we believe that 'knowledge and experience of the local communities'' would be a far more appropriate criterion to be applied to all candidates for the magistracy.

Disadvantage

To leave the issue of discrimination at this point would be to give a false impression of our findings. For we have not discussed a range of matters which, while not strictly within the narrow definition of discrimination set out in the Race Relations Act, have nevertheless created very real disadvantages for any black person wishing to become a magistrate. We must emphasise that many of these disadvantages are shared by white manual workers, for, in spite of the reforms over the last eighty years, the magistracy in England and Wales still remains peopled largely by the middle classes. The very concept of unpaid, part-time justices is tailored much more closely to the lives of professional people, the self-employed and those in public administrative positions than it is to the factory worker or labourer.

Even before the current recession it was difficult for manual workers to obtain permission from their firms to take a morning off every fortnight to sit on the Bench. It was a brave and probably foolish employee who would try and force the issue by quoting the Employment Protection (Consolidation) Act 1978 at his or her boss (see p.74). Moreover, the level of loss of earnings pay has never been high enough to compensate workers adequately for their actual loss in terms both of the deductions from their weekly wage packet and the adverse effect on their promotion prospects. Nowadays the employment situation and the very real threat of dismissal for workers who do not 'pull their weight' have considerably increased the risks and disadvantages of taking time off work to perform public duties. Black people suffer on average more than others in difficult times, not only because of racial prejudice in the labour market, but because they are over-represented in the ranks of unskilled and semi-skilled manual workers, the classes most vulnerable to the effects of economic recession.[41] Not surprisingly, many black manual workers who have a job are reluctant to do anything which might put their job at risk. Nor is it surprising that A.C. and S.C. representatives should complain of the lack of black, working-class candidates for the Bench.

Yet the dearth of black candidates is not simply the result of the economic situation and the demands involved in being a magistrate. The bias towards mainstream politics and public service inherent in the selection system also play their part in discouraging or failing to encourage black people from applying to join the Bench. Only a small proportion of black people join the mainstream political parties and an even smaller proportion are active in local or national party politics.[42] Moreover, many of those who might make very suitable J.P.s simply may not belong to committees or move in social circles where they would be likely to meet local politicians or existing magistrates (see p.43), the main sources of recruitment for the Bench. Furthermore, without people known and respected by the local 'establishment' to act as sponsors and proposers, and respected referees to support their application, their chances of success are probably reduced.

In the selection process itself many black people seemed to suffer from the disadvantage of 'not being known'. This may well have resulted in black candidates being rejected without interview at Branston and Harley, even when the official policy at Harley was to interview every candidate. The fact that many black candidates were 'unknown quantities', combined with the often haphazard, inadequate and unreliable ways in which enquiries were conducted into their 'suitability', meant that these candidates' interview performance probably took on an importance which it did not have for candidates who had acquaintances among local politicians, the magistracy and people involved in 'public service'. This, in itself, would not give cause for complaint if the interviews provided a fair and accurate assessment of each candidate's ability to perform adequately on the Bench, but, as we have already indicated, this was far from being the case. Not only do we differ from those who operate the selection process in mistrusting interviews undertaken by untrained and often unskilled interviewers, but we also regard the sort of formal interviews used by many A.C.s as being unfair to black, and particularly to Asian, candidates.

Panel interviews, in our view, give an advantage to those, such as teachers and members of committees, who have experience in appearing before others in a formal setting to answer questions and defend their opinions. They place at a disadvantage those who have no such experience, expecially those whose nerves and lack of confidence prevent them from giving a good account of themselves. They also place at a disadvantage those whose first language is not English and who may therefore have difficulty in projecting their personal qualities. Nor do we accept the argument that this combination of nerves and lack of confidence in self-expression within the formal interview necessarily means that the candidate will be unsuitable to sit as a magistrate. Black people may suffer from the additional disadvantage that these interviews are conducted almost exclusively by panels of white men and women. It was clear from our discussions with those Asians and Afro-Caribbeans who had stood as candidates that for some black candidates the subjective experience of being interviewed by white people was very different to that of white candidates in a similar situation. Unfortunately, we were unable to detect any sensitivity among the majority of selectors to a possible differential effect of interviews depending upon the race, colour and cultural background of interviewers and candidates.

Part 3:

MAGISTRATES AND BLACK PEOPLE

Chapter 12

PORTRAIT OF THE BLACK MAGISTRACY

'I don't see any harm in being middle class myself . . . I would like to see a random sample of wage-earners . . . this I have failed to do.'

(Lord Hailsham,
interview for ITV's 'The Law Machine' 1983)

Numbers of Black Magistrates

From the results of our survey there is no doubt that the total number of black magistrates in England and Wales has increased steadily over the past six years. We found that 62 per cent of black magistrates in the sixty-one petty sessional divisions (P.S.D.s) which answered our questionnaire were appointed since 1977. Moreover, almost a third had become J.P.s after the beginning of 1980. As Figure 3 shows, this represents a rate of increase in recruitment over the five years to 1983 which exceeds that for the magistracy as a whole by about 30 per cent. Even though our sample did not cover every Bench in the country, our figure of 119 very recent appointments of black magistrates indicates a substantial increase on the only other estimate of black appointments, that of Skyrme (1979), who states, without mentioning any source, that eighty black people were appointed to the Bench between 1962 and 1971.

As might be expected in the light of the information we acquired about the different methods and different attitudes of A.C.s and their secretaries with regard to the selection of black justices, there was no consistent pattern over the whole country, although there was at least one black person on the Bench in forty-eight out of the sixty-one Benches surveyed. On some Benches the rise in the number of black magistrates appointed had been sharp and sudden. In one Midlands city, for example, nine of the eleven black J.P.s were appointed between 1981 and 1983. In another Bench, in the North West, four out of five sitting black magistrates took

Figure 3   Number of years served on the bench by magistrates.

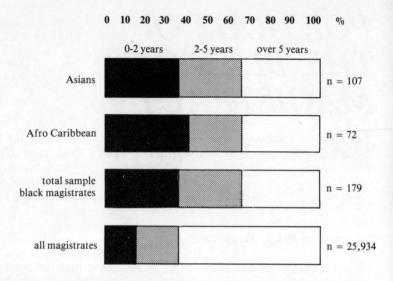

Note: Four Afro-Caribbean and nine Asian magistrates were not included because of incomplete information on questionnaire return.

office during that same period. In Branston, five out of the seven joined the Bench since 1980. The overall number of black magistrates traced through our postal survey are set out in Table 7 and identified according to gender and racial background. It is fair to assume that our sample is representative of the black magistracy as a whole, as it covers all the major areas where there is a substantial black population except Inner London, North-East London and Wolverhampton, which refused to complete our questionnaire.

Table 7: Total Black Magistrates According to Gender and Racial Background

	Male	Female	Total
West Indian/African	58	18	76
Asian	94	22	116
TOTAL	152	40	192

Two interesting facts emerged from this survey. In the first place, it is clear that there are substantially more Asian than Afro-Caribbean magistrates despite the language problems which many selectors identified as a major handicap for Asian candidates. Secondly, a much smaller proportion of the black magistracy were women (20.8 per cent) than in the magistracy as a whole, where in 1982 female J.P.s made up 42 per cent of the Bench (Cooke, 1984). The number of Asian women was particularly small, constituting only 19 per cent of all Asian magistrates.

Proportional Representation

Despite the increase in black appointments, ethnic communities remain substantially under-represented on local magistrates' Benches. We found that in most areas the numerical importance of black communities in the local population was not reflected in black membership of the Bench. Some of the greatest disparities were in P.S.D.s with the largest number of black magistrates. One example is a P.S.D. in the Midlands where the number of black magistrates has risen from two to eleven in the last two years. These appointments now put the proportion of black people on the Bench at 6.5 per cent, whereas the estimated black population was over 20 per cent. As Figure 4 indicates, we were able to make comparisons of this sort, not only for our five local study areas, but also in respect of twenty P.S.D.s covered by our survey where the boundaries coincided with those of the local census district. Overall, we found that in twenty-three of the twenty-five areas black people were inadequately reflected on the Bench, given their numbers in the local population. Moreover, in eighteen of these areas, even if the proportion of black magistrates were doubled, it would still fail to reflect the numbers of black people who lived in the area.

There were, however, two exceptions to this general pattern of under-representaton. One is a small Bench to the west of London (P.S.D.10) which has only forty-two magistrates. Of these, two are Asian and one Afro-Caribbean and together they constitute over 7 per cent of the magistrates in a town where the incidence of black people in the local population is just over 6 per cent. Another exception is a Bench with just under eighty magistrates on the southern fringe of London which covers an area where black, predominantly Asian, people make up 3 per cent of the population. The appointment of two Asians to the Bench in the last two years has put the proportion of black magistrates on the Bench at almost 4 per cent.

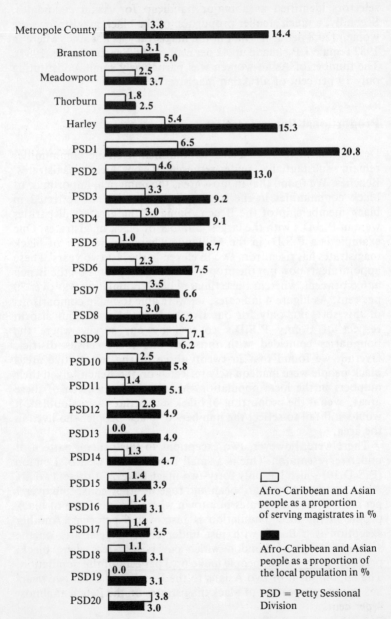

Figure 4   Afro-Caribbean and Asian people as a proportion of the local population and of serving magistrates.

Metropole County   3.8   14.4
Branston   3.1   5.0
Meadowport   2.5   3.7
Thorburn   1.8   2.5
Harley   5.4   15.3
PSD1   6.5   20.8
PSD2   4.6   13.0
PSD3   3.3   9.2
PSD4   3.0   9.1
PSD5   1.0   8.7
PSD6   2.3   7.5
PSD7   3.5   6.6
PSD8   3.0   6.2
PSD9   7.1   6.2
PSD10   2.5   5.8
PSD11   1.4   5.1
PSD12   2.8   4.9
PSD13   0.0   4.9
PSD14   1.3   4.7
PSD15   1.4   3.9
PSD16   1.4   3.1
PSD17   1.4   3.5
PSD18   1.1   3.1
PSD19   0.0   3.1
PSD20   3.8   3.0

☐ Afro-Caribbean and Asian
people as a proportion
of serving magistrates in %

■ Afro-Caribbean and Asian
people as a proportion of
the local population in %

PSD = Petty Sessional
Division

Social Background

The attempt by successive Lord Chancellors, their departmental officials and their A.C.s in recent years to give the magistracy the appearance of representing the whole community has, as we have seen, led to concern among selectors over the social composition of the magistracy. Much attention has, therefore, been paid to the class and occupation of magistrates. But there has been little or no concern over the true significance of class and occupation — that is the different attitudes of J.P.s towards the sort of issues which regularly come before the court and the extent to which their attitudes represent a cross-section of the local community.

In our study we tried to find out as much as possible about the social background of black magistrates and we were also concerned with their attitudes. As far as social class and occupation were concerned, we were able to compare our sample with previous studies of magistrates. This was of course not possible in the case of attitudes, but, we were able to make some comparisons between the views of the Asian and Afro-Caribbean J.P.s we interviewed and the members of the black communities whom we met during our local studies. We were also able to compare the attitudes of selection committee members to ascertain whether there was any truth in the criticism that selectors tend to choose similar people to themselves.

Survey Results

We found that the vast majority of black people on the Bench could be described as 'middle class' in that 159 out of 192 (82.8 per cent) were engaged in non-manual work. Moreover, there was a predominance of people from the 'higher professions', that is doctors, engineers, university lecturers (Registrar General's Social Class I) and from professions such as teaching, nursing, community work, and managerial posts in industry, local government and the civil service (Registrar General's Social Class II). At the other end of the occupational scale, the number of semi-skilled and unskilled manual workers was only thirteen, that is 6.8 per cent of the sample.

Compared with attempts by other researchers to analyse the occupational structure of magistrates, our results indicate that the class composition of black magistrates is very similar to that of the magistracy as a whole, as it was in 1966 at the time of Hood's (1972) research and in 1971/2 when John Baldwin (1976) surveyed all those recently appointed to the Bench. In view of the recent drive by the Lord Chancellor's Department and many A.C.s to recruit more 'working-class magistrates', however, one would perhaps expect an up-to-date survey of the social composition of the magistracy to show an increase in the number and proportion of manual workers on the Bench. If this is in fact the case, then black magistrates would appear to be more 'middle class' than their white colleagues. In the absence of any recent statistics on the magistracy as a whole, all we can reliably say is that the black magistracy is drawn from those social classes which have traditionally provided the country's J.P., since the abolition of the property qualification in 1907.

Table 8: Occupational Class of Black Magistrates
[See i. and ii.]

Registrar General's Classification		Afro-Caribbean	Asian	Total	%
i.	Higher Professional	12 [see iii]	39	51	26.6
ii.	Other Professional and Managerial	29	58	87	45.3
iii.	Other Non-Manual	11	10	21	10.9
	Skilled Manual	11	4	15	7.8
iv.	Semi-skilled Manual	9	3	12	6.3
v.	Unskilled Manual	1 [see iv]	0	1	0.5
	Unemployed	1	0	1	0.5
	Unknown	2	2	4	2.1
		76	116	192	100.00

Notes
   i. Women magistrates in employment are classified according to their occupation. Those not in employment are classified according to their husband's occupation.
  ii. Where the information provided by court officials was such that the precise occupation of a magistrate was unclear, we classified the magistrate in the lowest appropriate occupational class.
 iii. Includes one magistrate retired from work who is classified according to his previous occupation.
  iv. Described as 'shop-floor worker'.

What we have so far ignored in our analysis, however, are any differences that may exist between the class and occupational distribution of black and white people. If many more black people than white people are in manual occupations, then a black magistracy of predominantly middle-class people will be less representative of the black population as a whole than its white counterpart. The only recent statistics on the occupational

Figure 5   Non-manual and manual worker magistrates among black magistrates and according to previous research results

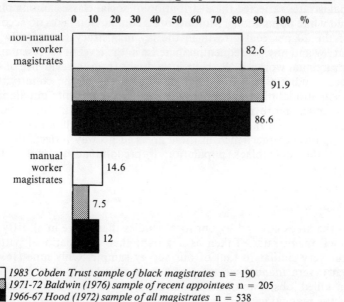

0   10   20   30   40   50   60   70   80   90   100 %

non-manual worker magistrates — 82.6, 91.9, 86.6

manual worker magistrates — 14.6, 7.5, 12

1983 Cobden Trust sample of black magistrates n = 190
1971-72 Baldwin (1976) sample of recent appointees n = 205
1966-67 Hood (1972) sample of all magistrates n = 538

distribution of black and white people appears in table 425 of the Labour Force Survey of 1981. From this survey it is clear that the percentage of black people in manual jobs is considerably greater than for the white population. The total percentage of white manual workers is given as 50.6 per cent, while for West Indians, Indians and Pakistani/Bangladeshis these percentages are 67.7 per cent, 59.3 per cent and 69 per cent respectively. Moreover, whereas non-manual workers account for almost half the white working population, for West Indians and Pakistani/Bangladeshis this figure is close to 30 per cent, and for Indians, 40 per cent. This means, in effect, that if black and white J.P.s were to be obtained from a cross-section of their respective populations the proportion of black working-class magistrates would exceed that of white working-class magistrates by between 10 and 20 per cent. Figure 5 in fact shows that when our sample is compared with the results of Hood's (1972) and Baldwin's (1976) surveys, the difference between the proportions of working-class magistrates is 2.5 per cent and 7.1 per cent respectively, i.e., much less than one would

105

expect if there were proportional class representation and less than one would expect if the ratio of working-class to middle-class magistrates reflected the distribution of social classes among black and white populations. Moreover this comparison takes no account of the 20 per cent growth in the lay magistracy since Baldwin's survey and any consequential increase in the level of representation for manual workers. We have little doubt from the evidence of our local studies (see below) that in some areas of the country, the occupational differences between the black and white populations are much more pronounced than those set out in the national statistics while the proportion of black working-class magistrates appointed to the Bench in these areas in no way reflects the fact that the local black population is predominantly employed in manual work.

Local Studies

In the areas covered by our local studies there were in all fifty-six black magistrates. Taken as a group, their occupational pattern was very similar to that of our survey sample. Only nine (16 per cent) were manual workers, of whom five had skilled and four unskilled jobs. Two of the five Benches in our study account for six of the manual workers, with Meadowport having as many as four out of their six black magistrates. In Harley and Metropole, however, the black members of the Bench were drawn almost exclusively from professional, managerial and other white-collar occupations. One Afro-Caribbean magistrate who sits on one of the Metropole petty sessional division Benches commented, 'I meet some ordinary white magistrates, but I don't know any ordinary black magistrates. All the black magistrates I know are professional people.' This is not surprising, since of the twenty-eight black magistrates in Metropole County only one has a manual job. The situation is little different at Harley, a city with a large population of Asian manual workers. Of the twelve black magistrates on the Harley Bench, only one is a manual worker and he is not Asian.

There has been some upward occupational mobility among the thirty-one black magistrates we met during the course of our research. However, the number who had made the transition into 'middle-class' occupations was nevertheless small, one Asian and three Afro-Caribbeans. Two other Asian magistrates had obtained university degrees before emigrating from their homeland, but had to accept manual jobs when they first arrived in England, one working in a textile factory for six months after his arrival. Our interviews with black magistrates suggested, therefore, that some of the 'middle-class' representatives might have had more experience of manual work than their class classification might indicate. However, such 'middle-class' black magistrates with manual work experience were not numerous.

Involvement in Public Life

All of the thirty-one black magistrates whom we interviewed were, or had at one time been, active in at least one area of local public life. The two main sorts of organisations to which they belonged were mainstream political parties and inter-racial community bodies. Their involvement in local politics encompassed, for instance, sitting on the council, being a school governor or holding office at ward or constituency level. In all, almost 60 per cent of our interview sample were involved in a local political organisation. Many of the magistrates in our interview sample were also involved in Afro-Caribbean or Asian organisations with specifically cultural interests, such as Asian literary societies or religious institutions, such as the mosque or temple. However, it was through their participation in local matters which involved both black and white people, rather than through their involvement in black community organisations, that they were likely to come into contact with magistrates or with other people who first suggested to them that they might join the Bench. In most cases this was through a specific organisation involving both black and white participation, such as a political party, police liaison committees, or the C.R.C.. Otherwise the contact was made through the black person's activity in some interest group, such as a West Indian Association which represented a particular section of the black community in local affairs.

The link between involvement in certain types of local activity and the recruitment of black people to the magistracy can best be illustrated by individual examples drawn from the five areas of our local study.

1. Asian Community Worker who frequently visited the courts with clients and commented on the lack of Asian magistrates. Persuaded to apply, after initial reluctance, by a senior community relations officer, who organised her application. Two politically active J.P.s, one Labour, one Conservative, were the referees. The magistrate was a member of neither party.
2. Afro-Carribean, works in local government. Involved in local Caribbean Association and an executive member of local C.R.C. On committee of constituency Labour Party. Approached by a friend who was also active in the Labour Party and was a magistrate. Was put forward as a Labour Party nominee.

3. Asian. Works in Community Relations. Chairman of Asian organisation. Member of Family Practitioners Committee, local Citizens Advice Bureau management committee, governing body of University. Asked many times to apply by executive members of local C.R.C., other white J.P.s and prominent Asians. Reluctant to do so because of pressure of work but eventually agreed. Referees were prominent people in local affairs.

4. Asian. Works as a senior engineer in a large company. Involved with local Scout Movement, also local Round Table and Rotary Club. Approached by white J.P. whom he knew because their sons went to the same school and who also worked in engineering and had heard of him before they met.

5. Asian. Works in Higher Education. Member of Advisory Committee to a Government Department. Deputy Chairmen of the Regional Electricity Consumer Council. Director of local radio station. Member of the Labour Party. He was approached through Labour Party circles and was put forward as a Labour Party nominee.

6. Afro-Caribbean. Has semi-skilled job. Very involved in community work through his church. Secretary of church community relations sub-committee. Chairman of local council of Christian churches. Member of C.R.C. Executive. School governor. Member of the liaison Committee. Approached by his church minister.

7. Afro-Caribbean. Skilled worker. Served in army. Life-long involvement with local youth clubs. Labour voter but more active involvement followed appointment to the Bench. Approached by a leading local politician who is also a senior magistrate to whom he was known both socially and through his youth work.

8. Afro-Caribbean. Skilled worker. Served in RAF. Very involved in Labour Party and Trade Union. Also active in charities and the church. A member of many committees. School governor. Deputy Chairman of local C.R.C.. Member of police liaison committee. Approached 'out of the blue' after a meeting with a J.P. active in Labour Party circles who was a member of three or four of the same committees. His referees were a politician and a minister, both well-known locally, and his application was endorsed by his local Labour Party and Trades Union branch.

The last three examples indicate that for working-class as well as middle-class black magistrates the involvement in local affairs seems to have been the all-important factor which led to their applications and eventual selection.

It is also interesting to note that very few of our interview sample either initiated their own application or had any desire to join the Bench before someone else put the idea into their head. They gave the impression that becoming a magistrate had been something that had happened to them rather than something that they had made happen.

I belonged to an Anglo-Afro-Caribbean organisation where there was a J.P. and he had been trying for ten years to get me to apply. But the demands of bringing up children and running a home, and my job and other activities had led me to refuse until about four years ago when the children were off my hands. (Afro-Caribbean magistrate)

One of the senior probation officers asked if I would like my name to go forward. At that time I refused as I wanted to spend time on my work. That was my only reason. Six or more years later the same friend made the suggestion again. When approached I felt personally indifferent. But by that time people had told me of unfair treatment by the police and by the court. I wanted to see how realistic this picture of magistrates and the police was, so I let my name go forward. (Asian magistrate).

The local MP suggested I should go forward. At that time it was not something I had given any thought to and I let the suggestion pass. Two years later the chairman of a hospital management committee on which I sat, who was also a senior J.P. in a neighbouring division, repeated the suggestion. As I had been making suggestions about having more black J.P.s at the time I therefore felt I had to let my name go forward. (Afro-Caribbean magistrate).

My appointment was accidental. I didn't know the procedure. Indigenous population members of _____ C.R.C. executive recommended me to be a magistrate. I wan't moved one way or another. _____ C.R.C. had indigenous members who were magistrates . . . I was proposed by active political people, one Labour and one Tory, both prominent. (Afro-Caribbean magistrate)

Some who eventually became magistrates resisted initial invitations to put their names forward because of the demands of their work or family life. One refused at first for political reasons.

For the majority, however, the idea of joining the Bench simply had not occurred to them.

Attitudes

Appointment of Black Magistrates

Our interviews with black J.P.s tended to concentrate on their personal background and the way in which they found themselves on the Bench. The interviews, however, also covered the general subject of the need for black magistrates. There was a small number of respondents for whom this was not even an issue worth discussing. As far as they were concerned, magistrates were magistrates and the colour of their skin was immaterial. They tended to be those black magistrates who had little or no contact with other black people.

A few of those who did have contact with their local black community were very ambivalent about colour being emphasised as they feared this might foster or perpetuate patronising attitudes. We were told, for example, by one such magistrate, 'I would be insulted if it was mentioned that I am a magistrate only because I am coloured. I would prefer to point out what I have got to offer the magistracy or what active role I can play as a magistrate.' (Afro-Caribbean J.P., Thorburn). One Asian J.P. followed his reply that he would not like to see any more or any less Asians on the Bench, but 'people who are suited to become magistrates' with the comment, 'If the aim is to improve race relations, this should . . . be done in areas other than the magistracy, for example, the police and in housing.' This sentiment was echoed, but for different reasons, by an Indian magistrate who believed that having more Asian J.P.s was not the best way to help the Asian community. He told us that there was a danger of greatly over-emphasising the usefulness of magistrates to black communities because 'magistrates are bound by certain norms and have a very small area of discretion'.

Nevertheless, most of the magistrates we interviewed at least gave their support to the idea that there should be more black people on the Bench. One Asian magistrate specified four reasons for appointing black J.P.s. These are:
1. It helps black people accept the institutions of mainstream society.
2. It helps self-esteem.
3. It helps young members of the black community by providing positive role models.
4. It help white people to see black people in authority.

110

Another reason mentioned by some black J.P.s was a possibility that black appointments might have a beneficial psychological effect on the community. As stated more specifically by one of them: 'A Bench composed of different races has a long-term desirable effect on people's attitude towards members of the coloured community. It is the recognition of people as useful members of society which makes the coloured community acceptable.'

Others saw the need for black J.P.s in terms of political democracy, and the ideal of all sectors of society being adequately represented on the Bench. The legitimacy argument that we had heard so often from selectors was also repeated by one Asian magistrate who told us that the (Asian) community cannot claim to be treated unjustly when Sikhs and other Asians are on the Bench.

Yet the majority of black magistrates to whom we spoke did not mention either political or social reasons for increasing their numbers on the Bench, but referred rather to what might be termed 'judicial reasons', that is related to the magistrate's courtroom functions. Some of them spoke of ways in which their cultural background enabled them to 'understand' black defendants in court better than their white colleagues. This understanding often took the form of acting as a language interpreter, even where the defendant's first language was English. 'Colleagues will say, "Mr [Jones], would you mind explaining what the defendant meant by saying this", and you explain it to them.' (Afro-Caribbean Magistrate). It also involved providing their white colleagues with information about the customs and cultural characteristics of black people.

I think my presence has helped the Bench in relation to the way black people act and react to certain pressures. (Afro-Caribbean magistrate)

When it comes to West Indians having loud parties and going on to six o'clock in the morning and all those things, I can understand that . . . It is very difficult for an English magistrate to understand it. (Afro-Caribbean magistrate)

A number of magistrates regarded their presence as likely to increase the confidence of a black defendant that he or she would get a 'fair trial'. 'I felt that it would be of some help to West Indians and Asians in Court that if justice was administered by people from the same background, they would feel less unjustly treated.' (Afro-Caribbean magistrate).

111

In particular, three magistrates suggested that the presence of a black person on the bench might reduce any fear black defendants had of the court. Describing his own experience, one of them said: 'I believe my presence reassures some defendants. I can see the look of recognition and sometimes surprise when they see me on the Bench.' (Afro-Caribbean magistrate).

The possibility of black magistrates acting as a safeguard against discrimination by white members of the Bench, was mentioned by four magistrates.

I feel very much that my presence on the Bench makes a difference. It's not my views that make a difference, my presence inhibits them. (Asian magistrate)

I keep an eye open and an ear listening to hear the type of comments made by Tory colleagues, whether they might be racial. (Afro-Caribbean magistrate)

Two of these magistrates thought black magistrates could counteract any tendency to reach conclusions as a result of the stereotyping of black people by white magistrates.

The pressure of more black magistrates can only have a good effect . . . I have encountered too many magistrates who adopt a stereotyped approach. I get the impression they make up their minds long before the case is over. (Afro-Caribbean magistrate)

I hear it sometimes' [from white magistrates], 'these Rastafarians, they're always in trouble', but they haven't even heard the cases yet. The fact that this is so doesn't enter into it . . . [But] this sort of tendency is declining now, and if I have contributed a little to that declining I would be quite pleased. (Afro-Caribbean magistrate)

Also, it was noticeable that, while some magistrates were aware that their presence on the Bench could make a difference to the court's decisions, and that, to quote one Afro-Caribbean J.P., 'Fairness of treatment may be affected by the individual magistrates on the Bench', only six appeared to have made the connection between differences in cultural background and experience and differences in attitude which could affect decision-making in the manner which we described in the second chapter of this report. Of these magistrates, three suggested specifically that their 'black perspective', might influence sentencing decisions of the Bench. One of them said, 'I've been able to explain customs and practices of West Indians which magistrates weren't aware of and, therefore, been able to mitigate, in some cases, penalties which were going to be harsher.' (Afro-Caribbean magistrate). Two other magistrates each mentioned a case in which their cultural knowledge had influenced the verdict of the court. An Asian magistrate told us that his informing his fellow magistrates that an Asian lady arrested for shoplifting might be divorced if found guilty had led to her being given a conditional discharge. Another Asian magistrate recounted influencing colleagues on the Bench to regard an incident in which the victim was Asian not as 'boys having fun on Friday night' but as racial harassment.

Perhaps one reason why connecting differences in cultural background and experience with decision-making in court did not occur more often among black magistrates was that it conflicted so sharply with the official ideology of 'objective' decision-making (see p.7). Only one magistrate, an Afro-Caribbean, touched directly upon this issue when he said: 'If there is a doubt, you're supposed to give it to them [Afro-Caribbean defendants]. You will understand a doubt better than an English magistrate. As I say, it might be false, but that's the presumption that they [Afro-Caribbean defendants] have.'

What we found was relatively lacking among the black magistrates — compared to many black non-magistrates we interviewed — was the sense that black people are engaged in a struggle for social, political and economic equality with the indigenous white population and that their own presence and the presence of other black magistrates on the Bench might be a step to achieving such equality. Only one black J.P., for example, explicitly mentioned the collective struggle of black people for political power which occupies the thoughts and writings of many black people today. According to this Asian J.P., 'We are fighting for a share of power. The whole thing is about power. We can't have it both ways . . . As many black people as white get into a position of power and redress the balance socially in terms of policies and resources, so much the better.'

There was rather more frequent mention of the importance of individual black people attaining positions of authority and public office. Different magistrates highlighted different areas of political and economic life as targets for black advancement. Amongst the targets they cited were Member of Parliament, judges, local government, both councillors and officers, and the professions. A few did link the relative lack of black people in positions of authority and public office with the shortage of black magistrates. For example, an Afro-Caribbean J.P. commenting on the comparatively small number of black magistrates said, 'It is one of the many frustrations the black community has to fight against.'

However, for the majority of magistrates who explicitly expressed a wish to see black people enjoying greater equality, it seemed equality had more to do with personal dignity and gaining respect from white people than with black people achieving power in their own right. This desire for recognition was clear for example, from an anecdote told to us by one black magistrate: 'When I went to court one day the policewoman saw me moving towards the magistrates' room. She said, "You can't go in there, it's for magistrates", so I turned to her and said, "Well, I am a magistrate".'

The Selection Process and Black People

We asked the black J.P.s we interviewed to comment not only on their own experience of being selected as a magistrate, but also on how they saw the selection process in general and its treatment of black candidates. Although any statistical breakdown of the replies we received would be meaningless because of the small numbers involved, the impression we formed was, firstly, that most black magistrates had little detailed knowledge of the criteria used in selecting and appointing J.P.s, but, secondly, that on the basis of their own experience, there was no reason to believe that the selection procedure operates unfairly for black people. Only about 20 per cent of the black magistrates we talked to criticised the recruitment procedure which had resulted in the comparatively few black magistrates on their local Benches. Those who were critical of the system that had appointed them tended to direct their attack at what they saw as the class bias of the selectors rather than specifically against any racist attitudes. Thus according to one Asian J.P.,

If British institutions in general have not drawn on their own working class satisfactorily, it would be rash to expect them to draw in from outside people who come from different races, cultural and religious . . . White working classes suffer from this kind of prejudice and discrimination and attitudes too . . .

One Afro-Caribbean magistrate saw this class bias as placing additional obstacles in the path of most black candidates: 'The sort of people who get proposed are likely to be professional types, because the committee are mainly professional types. West Indians do not have access to professional organisations.'

This same magistrate also believed that the strong political influence in the selection system might exclude Caribbeans because

114

'many West Indians are not interested in politics'.

Yet the link between party politics and the Bench was defended by another Asian J.P. who claimed that, 'You get more experience in life and community through political activity than through anything else.'

Another aspect of the selection system which came in for criticism was the emphasis on voluntary-work experience, which was seen by one Asian magistrate as a factor which tended to exclude working-class blacks and whites, as voluntary work was very much 'a middle-class concept'.

The stress on confidentiality and a lack of information were further aspects of the present procedures which were criticised by one Afro-Caribbean J.P. for their likely reduction of chances of black people being recruited. 'By its very nature, it [the recruitment process] will operate against people who don't know how it works. The host community is not going out of its way to inform the ethnic minorities.'

Many of the points that we ourselves have made in this report about the idiosyncrasies of the selection process and the criteria for recommendation were picked up by a number of black J.P.s. Generally, however, we found that those black magistrates who offered any critical comments were in the minority of our sample and those who were willing and able to direct their criticism to specific issues could be counted on the fingers of one hand.

Constructive comments on how the system could be improved were similarly few. There were a number of suggestions for more openness. One was for the names of all A.C. members to be published, so that it would be possible to examine their past attitudes towards racial issues. Another J.P. wanted to ensure that the A.C. membership reflected the population of the particular area for which they were responsible. A further suggestion was that the Lord Chancellor should circulate a directive to A.C.s, instructing them to seek out black people for appointment to the Bench. However, most of the comments on possible changes to the system went no further than calls for greater availability of information about how to apply, and for, as one Afro-Caribbean J.P. put it, 'the net to be spread wider'.

Although one or two of our interview sample expressed the hope that they might influence the recruitment process in a similar way to their influence on decision-making — by putting on pressure for change from within — there was a general feeling of frustration and inevitability running through the magistrates' criticism of the present system. This is best summarised by quotations from an Asian and an Afro-Caribbean who sit on Benches in different parts of the country. According to the Asian J.P., the present system was so hierarchical and so firmly in the grip of the conservative element at the top that no radical changes were possible 'without a well-organised external movement'. He was convinced that those within the system, even people with a radical political background were not going to change it, because 'they became part of it'. The Afro-Caribbean magistrate also emphasised the general conservatism of the system and its imperviousness to change.

> They don't want people to come here and start rocking the boat. It's very select — no, that's not the correct word — but it's very conservative. I mean they'll try their best to leave the system as it is . . . Change there is very, very difficult . . . The die-hards . . . it's like a rock.

Another Afro-Caribbean J.P. considered that external pressure alone would be counter-productive as the authorities would then take up entrenched positions. As he saw it only a two-pronged movement, external and internal had any hope of bringing about change: 'The more you attack them from the outside, the more they will resist. Change can only come by a combination of issues being raised outside and people inside raising these issues with their colleagues.'

A small number of our interview sample thought the recruitment process was changing. An Asian J.P. believed there was now a much more open approach to appointments than when he was recruited some five years earlier, and supported his claim by drawing attention to newspaper articles which had recently appeared giving information about the magistracy and how to apply. Another Asian magistrate commented, 'We are being considered for appointment now, whereas we weren't twenty years ago.' An Afro-Caribbean magistrate who is a manual worker believed that although his Bench tended to be 'upper-middle-class people . . . not knowing how ordinary people live' the system is changing. His own appointment, he suggested, was evidence of change for, 'twenty years ago I wouldn't even have been approached.'

The Qualities Needed for a Magistrate

Perhaps it is not surprising that when asked what qualities they would wish to see in a magistrate, the majority of our sample answered in the same vague general terms that we had heard from A.C. and S.C. representatives — 'commonsense', 'the judicial mind', 'a balanced view', 'an analytical mind', 'experience of life in all possible ways'. For some of the black J.P.s, 'experience of

116

life in all possible ways' included having some awareness of the pressures which shape the lives of economically disadvantaged people, both black and white. The importance of this quality was usually expressed as criticism of some or most of their fellow J.P.s and can be illustrated by a brief quote from an Afro-Caribbean magistrate who had strong views on this issue: '[Magistrates] should be exposed to people who suffer real disadvantage. A lot of them haven't a bloody clue what poverty and suffering is . . . middle-class attitudes and values predominate.'

Some of the black J.P.s expressed the belief that specific knowledge of their own cultural and racial group was also important.

> You must have knowledge of how people with West Indian backgrounds, for example, actually live, their way of life. (Afro-Caribbean J.P., Harley)

> Knowledge of the local community when you're sitting on judgement of those from the same community. (Asian J.P., Metropole County)

As we have already mentioned, several black magistrates saw this knowledge as justifying the presence of black magistrates on the Bench insofar as it increases the efficiency of the court by providing interpreters for defendants and offering white members of the Bench some insight into cultural and religious behaviour of ethnic minorities. A small minority of our sample, however, perceived such knowledge and experience as positive attributes in themselves, attributes which could actually affect decision-making. One described lay magistrates as having 'inbuilt pre-judgement'. His own pre-judgement, coming as it did from a different background and a different part of society, could help to balance that of middle-class white people. Another spoke of his ability to use his influence on the Bench 'to persuade other magistrates to see things in a different way'. For another, knowledge of cultural background was irrelevant in criminal cases, but could be useful in the domestic or juvenile court.

> I can't see how cultural background could be a mitigation for someone charged with burglary. In civil cases cultural background may be taken into account in many cases, for example, an auntie exercising the role of a parent is very common in Asian families. (Asian J.P., Harley)

One black magistrate, however, did express doubts as to whether the generation who grew up abroad before emigrating to Britain did in fact have an accurate understanding of the generation who had grown up in this country. 'I've lost touch. I don't know what the current trends are, how the young people are behaving now, what is acceptable. I probably still judge it by my time in Trinidad.' (Afro-Caribbean J.P.). He went on to suggest that 'what is needed is young black people on the Bench to bring it up-to-date'.

Some black magistrates saw personal characteristics as having an important bearing on whether black J.P.s would actually try to bring their knowledge of their communities to bear on the work of magistrates' courts. This issue was touched on by an Asian J.P. who commented, 'If we are to have only tokens they want to be strong tokens'. Another Asian J.P. suggested that if black J.P.s did not have a strong character they might be 'Uncle Toms'. A number of magistrates expressed a belief in their ability to put forward their views in a forthright manner and influence the Bench even if they were outnumbered by white people by two to one.

Only three magistrates in our sample mentioned a critical view of police behaviour as being a relevant attitude for J.P.s. One of them had been involved in an incident during which he thought the police had not behaved properly and as a result he had considered resigning from the Bench. He told us: 'Speaking as a magistrate, the magistrates do believe the police far too often.' (Afro-Caribbean magistrate). His views were echoed by another Afro-Caribbean magistrate who said 'for some magistrates everything the police say is bible'. A third magistrate had been involved in a complaint against the police at the time of his appointment — a fact that had not come out in his selection interview. In his opinion: '[The] majority of magistrates take the policeman's word, but I do know that they can lie, and until I have heard both the police and the defendant's story, and the police can really prove the case to me, I don't find people guilty.'

General Attitude

The conclusion we reached from our interviews with thirty-one black magistrates was that on the whole they were people who were very conscious of their position and of the responsibilities involved in sitting on the Bench. Some saw it as a great honour: 'Magistrates [are] top people with initials after their names. You have a feeling that you are able to offer something to them, and the great thing is that they accept it.' (Afro-Caribbean magistrate, Branston). Despite the confidentiality we assured them, our impression was that some were extremely cautious in what they said during their interviews. This cautious attitude was also evident in the fact that

118

several black magistrates mentioned to us that, after they became J.P.s, they had to be careful about what they said in public, 'especially if it can be termed controversial'.

We have perhaps tended to highlight in our examples those magistrates who expressed the most forthright criticisms of the composition of the Bench, their fellow J.P.s and the selection procedure. Yet we must re-emphasise that these magistrates were a minority of our interview sample. Even the more outspoken black J.P.s, while in tune with the aspirations of black people for economic, social and political advancement, tended to be committed to working within existing institutions to achieve these ends. What we noticed above all as a general characteristic of the black magistrates we interviewed was a lack of affinity with and sympathy for the aspirations of those black people who see the way forward for black communities in direct confrontation with white society in the political, economic and ideological arenas. Any notion of a collective struggle for power and an active fight against prejudice and discrimination which might involve bringing pressure to bear from outside the legal system in order to change that system and the way it operates in relation to black people was, it seems, far removed from the consciousness of almost all black people who sat on the magistrates' Bench.

Chapter 13

THE CONFIDENCE OF THE COMMUNITY

A recurring catchphrase in our discussions with members of the Lord Chancellor's Department and Advisory and Sub-Committee representatives was 'the confidence of the community'. The community, we were told, had confidence in the magistracy and magistrates' courts. People who had spoken out against the police, 'extremists', people with recent convictions for motoring offences, or who had recently been divorced, could not be appointed to the Bench, for to do so would be to risk losing 'the confidence of the community'.

Yet, as far as we are aware, no attempt has been made to gauge in a systematic way whether this belief that people have confidence in magistrates is well-founded. The only survey to be carried out was that undertaken by the government's own Social Survey Division of the Office of Population Censuses and Surveys in 1974.[43] Although this survey related only to the views of defendants, who may not be representative of the community at large, the results gave little support to the argument that people have confidence in magistrates' courts. The study revealed that 'over two-thirds of defendants . . . who chose the venue for their trial agreed with the statement put to them that magistrates' courts were police courts', and the suggestion that a defendant always gets a fair trial in these courts was rejected by over half the defendants.[44] Moreover, it could not be argued that this was simply a matter of sour grapes by those who had been found guilty and sentenced by a bench of magistrates. Of those defendants who chose to go to the Crown Court and were not therefore tried by magistrates 35 per cent spontaneously mentioned as one of the reasons for their choice their belief that magistrates' courts were police courts.[45]

Confidence in the Magistrates

During the course of our own research we tried to find out how the black people we interviewed saw the magistrates, the present composition of the Bench and the selection process. Unlike the government's Social Survey Division, however, we did not direct our research at defendants' responses to magistrates courts, since we did not have the resources to include a sufficiently large sample of black defendants as part of our project. We, therefore, had to rely for our account of the black communities' view of magistrates' justice upon reports from C.R.C.s and from individual members of the black community whom we interviewed. The overall impression we obtained was that what went on in magistrates' courts was not a major concern among black people. This may well be because those individuals or groups most likely to be affected by magistrates' decisions did not voice their opinions of the courts to either C.R.C.s or to our black interviewees.

Of the twenty-nine (49 per cent) of C.R.C.s who replied to the question (contained in our postal questionnaire) relating to public concern about magistrates' attitudes to black people, twenty-three (79 per cent) stated that they had received complaints about the magistrates' courts, but only ten (34 per cent) maintained that these complaints were frequent or very frequent. The most frequent complaint made to C.R.C.s was that magistrates displayed a lack of sympathy for the views and culture of black people and made adverse value judgements in cases involving black defendants. Although their frequency was relatively small, it was particularly disturbing to discover that eight C.R.C.s had received complaints about racism, racial bias in sentencing and stereotyping at the hands of magistrates. As for complaints about the composition of the Bench, 69.5 per cent of all those fifty-nine C.R.C.s returning our questionnaire told us that they had received some complaints, but only eight (13.5 per cent) of them stated that these complaints were frequent or very frequent. To our question asking whether the C.R.C. had identified any public concern about the lack of black magistrates on the Bench only twelve (20 per cent) indicated that there had been some concern.

These figures tend to mask the strength of feeling against the local magistrates' court in some areas. Two C.R.C.s in particular stood out as being especially forceful in their criticisms of the magistrates. One from the London area wrote:

Magistrates are racially prejudiced. They are mainly upper class. They have a lot of predetermined views about black people. They always accept what the police say. They believe blacks are liars. Bail is given to blacks less readily than to whites. It's a police court.

The other C.R.C. in the West Midlands, listed the complaints it had received against the local magistrates as follows:

a. Not giving consideration to circumstances and the background of the defendant.
b. Blindly following and relying on the prosecution case.
c. Treatment given to defendants on occasions tends to amount to snubbing them.
d. Little attention paid to defendants' submissions outlining the mitigating circumstances.
e. Downright, open and naked racism.

When we put similar questions about the local Bench to the representatives of black organisations whom we interviewed, about half, mostly from Afro-Caribbean organisations, told us that they had received complaints about the magistrates' courts' treatment of black people. These complaints ranged from general dissatisfaction with the quality of justice in magistrates' courts — 'They're police courts'. 'Black people do not get a fair deal.' — to more specific charges, including, in two cases, accusations of racist behaviour against two particular magistrates. The secretary of an Asian organisation in Metropole told us that it had received complaints about the speed of cases, inconsistency in fines and a failure to appreciate the need for interpreters. Specific complaints about the composition of the Bench were rare with only six of our interviewees mentioning ever having received such a complaint. Two of these arose from the court's handling of a major public order incident, and it would seem that it is this sort of case rather than the routine fare of magistrates' courts which is likely to raise public awareness and give rise to questions about the Bench's composition.

The relatively few complaints received about the dearth of black magistrates cannot, however, be taken as indicating complete satisfaction with the composition of the local Bench. It simply would not occur to most people, defendants included, that there was anything they could do to influence the composition of the Bench.

The issue of black magistrates would . . . seem far removed from people's priorities . . . many people indicate that they cannot possibly have any influence on the judiciary. (C.R.C. questionnaire reply)

Local youth feel that the magistrates' set-up is beyond them. They don't know where they come from or how they're appointed. They don't meet them in the street. They don't complain because they don't have any contact with them. They consider that they can't have any effect on them, so they don't complain. (Chairperson, Afro-Caribbean organisation, Metropole County)

According to one community worker from Branston, this acceptance of the Bench's composition as immutable and inevitable might contain an element of the old colonial mentality — 'It's accepted that that's the way, because it happened in the West Indies, so why not in England? People who sat in judgement there were white.'

Yet it was not merely that black organisations had received few complaints from their members or the public about the composition of the Bench; these organisations themselves had for the most part not considered it to be an issue which required their attention. The question of black appointments to the Bench had, we found, been discussed either formally or informally in only about half these organisations. In Metropole County, where we had contact with a large number of representatives from Asian and Afro-Caribbean organisations, we learnt that in nine out of seventeen organisations the topic had never been raised even in passing. Moreover, only three of these organisations had put forward candidates for selection.

In most black organisations, therefore, the magistracy is of relatively low priority compared with other issues. As the chairman of an Asian organisation put it, 'It's important, but not important enough to get on the agenda.' This low priority was confirmed by a former officer of an active Asian group who said that from the late sixties onwards, 'We gave greater priority for representation on school boards, hospital management committees, social security tribunals . . . we didn't press for representation on magistrates' Benches.'

It is difficult to give any generally applicable reasons for this lack of interest, but the comments made by one Community Relations Officer may provide a clue.

It [the magistracy] is a British thing. It's away from us. I suppose they've never been really got at. It's only in very recent years that blacks have been beginning to get more involved or want to get more involved in public life. Now there are more black councillors than ever before. There's an emphasis on councillors, school governors or whether blacks should join the police. But I think being on the Bench was something we never graduated to. Maybe we felt it was beyond our reach.

The social distance, therefore, between black organisations and the magistrates' courts and the magistracy appears to be significantly greater than that between these organisations and other social institutions, such as schools, hospitals and local councils.

Confidence in the Selection Process

The first point to be made is that while almost all the representatives of black organisations to whom we spoke knew magistrates were not elected but appointed by 'a committee' and over half knew of the existence of the local A.C., only a minority had any detailed knowledge of the mechanics of the selection process. We found that some senior officers in black community organisations seemed to have only the vaguest idea about how the system worked, and, as the chairman of an Asian organisation remarked, 'If not even community leaders like myself know the procedure for recruiting and appointing magistrates, what chance have the ordinary people of knowing how to put their names forward?'

Two main reasons were offered to us to explain this state of affairs. First, there was the remoteness of the black communities from the selection process and the people who operate that process.

Just precisely what happens? I don't think people in the black community know very much about it. I think they feel it's mysterious, a magical thing. It's just mystique, and you've got to be a certain kind of person. (Community Relations Officer, Metropole County)

People don't know the whole area of these appointments, how it can be initiated, where best to contact people and so on. It's a matter of mental reference for the settler community. I think the settler community has not developed those references within the local population (Asian J.P., Metropole County)

Secondly, the Lord Chancellor's Department and the selection committees were seen as providing very little encouragement to black organisations to become involved in the selection process. In this regard the general notices sent out by A.C.s were seen by one black J.P. as an inadequate method of involving black people and their community organisations: 'Maybe until individuals and organisations are contacted specifically, to a large extent they see such notices as not applying to them' (Community Relations Officer, Branston). Indeed, a few of the interviewees involved in

124

black community organisations felt particularly frustrated at the lack of any approach from the local A.C.

> Organisations like us who do voluntary work and who have a group of people, feel that we can be of service and of assistance, but we have never been approached . . . I wouldn't like to say it is deliberate, but it does appear as if they tend to deliberately by-pass organisations like ours. (Chairman, Afro-Caribbean organisation, Metropole County)

Needless to state this lack of contact did not inspire confidence in the selection system amongst the black people we interviewed. In some cases it gave rise to the mistaken belief that the organisation was not entitled to put forward candidates.

> We have never been included by the Lord Chancellor. He has never written us a letter. We have not thought we are authorised to sponsor . . . I don't think there is a policy in the Lord Chancellor's Department to encourage and even accept sponsorship from community organisations . . . We understood we were not authorised to sponsor, therefore there was no desire on the part of the organisation to sponsor anybody for the magistracy. (Chairman, Asian organisation, Metropole County)

Among those who knew something about the selection process there was a widespread belief that only black people from certain groups were at all likely to be selected as J.P.s, 'I think they will always select middle-class people. Anyone they pick from the black community will be a middle-class person.' (Executive member, Afro-Caribbean organisation). It was also suggested that these black people had become distanced from the grass-roots of the local black community: 'Magistrates get recruited by a top pool of people. Any . . . Indian who gets considered through contacts with this network is likely to be unrepresentative because he will have moved away from his community.' (Secretary, Asian youth organisation, Metropole County)

There was also the feeling among several of those we interviewed that people who speak out against the police or against injustice are almost certain to be rejected. Some of the members of an Afro-Caribbean organisation had no doubt that the real reason behind the rejection of 'controversial' candidates was the committee's determination to exclude from the Bench anyone who might criticise the police. Other representatives of black organisations had similar comments to make about the generally cautious attitude of the selectors. 'The individual must be, according to their

125

notions and conceptions, a safe individual . . . The point I'm making is that those who have never uttered a word against the injustice that is being done [are appointed]. I have no confidence in him, that he will do justice.' (Chairman, C.R.C.) This belief that A.C.s and S.C.s take a very narrow view of who is 'acceptable' extended to proposing and acting as referee for a candidate. Some of our respondents felt, therefore, that for them to sponsor a candidate's application to become a J.P. would result inevitably in that candidate's rejection. 'My intention was to do so [sponsor], but I thought it would do a lot of damage to him.' Others believed that their sponsorship had actually been a handicap to candidates.

> As chairman of the C.R.C. I was in a position to recommend certain people and to me they were very competent and knew the language. I think they didn't accept them because I nominated them. I'm considered an outspoken person on matters which concern minorities' (Chairman, Harley C.R.C.)

We found that some organisations gave similar reasons for not putting forward candidates. Thus, an executive member of an Afro-Caribbean organisation in Metropole County told us, 'Candidates from some groups are more acceptable to the selection committee than candidates from other groups. I believe candidates from the . . . C.R.C. are more acceptable than candidates from [his organisation].

This lack of acceptance by the selectors was not, we were told by one black community worker, confined to black organisations,

> This C.A.B. is quite well-known all over the country. It's quite left-wing in its attitude. We're not a political party or politically motivated in any way, but we want the same rights as everybody and equality . . . That is known and because that is known it would be difficult for anyone from this C.A.B., black or white, to be appointed.

In fact two workers from this C.A.B., one black person and one white person, had stood as candidates for the magistracy and had been turned down.

Some of the representatives of black organisations to whom we spoke suggested that the surest way to be selected was through sponsorship by a political party. 'Anybody can recommend anybody, but eventually it gets back to the political circle before the person is finally accepted. Therefore it is probably easiest to become a magistrate if recommended by a political party.' (Member of Afro-Caribbean organisation, Metropole County)

In Branston the recent domination of the local political parties over the selection process, had not gone unnoticed. 'It was an open secret. The political parties dole it out' (Chairman C.R.C.). 'Tory and Labour parties operated a closed shop. They always nominated party members and they were not interested in co-opting black people.' (former community Relations Officer). Both these people agreed, however, that things had improved and it was now possible for black candidates who were not Party members to be appointed.

We found, particularly from our local study interviews, that there was often an important relationship between the decisions of the selectors in relation to certain black candidates and the subsequent attitude towards the selection committee of the organisations which had proposed the candidates. This 'feedback' effect was likely to be extremely negative when a well-known and well-liked member of the black community failed to be appointed, or where a number of black candidates was rejected. Indeed, several of the representatives of black community organisations and C.R.C.s to whom we spoke had become disillusioned after failures of candidates whom they had endorsed and they no longer thought it worthwhile to put forward names to the selection committee. Although there were also occasions when the appointment of a black candidate resulted in positive feedback and a significant increase in the number of black applicants for the local Bench, such occasions were, we found, rare. The only black community representatives in our five local study areas who were prepared to defend the present system of appointments and support its continuation without expressing any need for reform were existing magistrates, and even some of them were highly critical of certain aspects of the system's operation (see pp.114-6).

Two-thirds of the C.R.C.s who returned our questionnaire were also dissatisfied with the system for selecting J.P.s, while only 15 per cent were satisfied. Although the most common reason they gave for their dissatisfaction was that black community groups were not approached or provided with information, another major cause for complaint was that too few black people were appointed. One C.R.C. specifically attributed this failure on the part of the selectors to discrimination. 'We are not satisfied as we believe the process to be indirectly discriminatory, given the almost total absence of black magistrates covering [our area].' Six complained of the secrecy of the system. This secrecy combined with the lack of adequate representation of minority groups prompted two of these, one in the south-east and the other in the Midlands, to make highly critical comments about the system's operation. The former wrote, 'It appears very much like an old boys' network.' While the latter saw the system as being 'like a closed shop, very secretive, an old school network'. This C.R.C. also stated that the fact that the magistracy was part of the 'establishment' was the reason that black people did not put themselves foward for selection.

The critical comments of C.R.C.s about the selection process were very similar to those we had heard from representatives of black organisations, and as a whole, C.R.C.s seemed no more favourably disposed towards it than many black people we interviewed in our local studies. The C.R.C.s doubts about the equity of the selection process go some way towards explaining why, though they showed widespread concern about the low numbers of black people on their local Benches, they did not propose many candidates. Of the fifty-nine C.R.C.s who returned our questionnaire thirty (50.8 per cent) said the number of black people on their local Bench was 'much too low' and fifteen (8.5 per cent) stated it was 'too low'. Only five C.R.C.s (8.5 per cent) regarded the number of black J.P.s in their area as 'satisfactory'.[46] C.R.C.s also appear to consider having adequate black representation to be important for community relations. The majority of C.R.C.s in our survey thirty-eight (64.6 per cent) said it was 'very important' and fourteen others (23.7 per cent) said it was 'quite important'. Only one C.R.C. said it was 'irrelevant'.[47] Yet, our survey also revealed that less than half the C.R.C.s, twenty-six (44.1 per cent), had sponsored candidates between 1974 and 1982 and that of those who had, only a handful had put forward more than three people during the eight-year period.

Attitudes Towards Black Appointments to the Bench

It was our view that a reliable measure of the general confidence of the black community in the present system of lay magistrates, and the process by which they are selected, could be found in the attitude of black people towards the appointment of Asian and Afro-Caribbean magistrates. If black people supported unreservedly the appointment of more black J.P.s of the social class and background to those already sitting on the Bench, then this would indicate confidence both in the magistracy and in the selection process with the minor reservation that the number of black appointments was insufficient — a defect easily enough remedied by the selectors without any fundamental changes to the present system. If, however, there were some indication from members of the black community that a policy of 'more of the same' would not in their view improve matters, this would imply that far more radical changes would be necessary in order to win the confidence of most black people.

The only clear result on this issue from our local studies was that there was a very wide range of opinion. Some of our informants did indeed support unreservedly the idea of having more black people on the Bench. The reasons they gave were very similar to those suggested to us by black magistrates. However, several of the people we interviewed, while supporting the general notion of more black J.P.s, nevertheless had serious doubts about the system of selection. For example, an executive member of an Afro-Caribbean organisation spelt out three reasons why he favoured the appointment of black people to the Bench. These were (1) to build up the influence of the black communities over the courts; (2) to help to ensure that a black defendant is tried on the same basis as a white defendant and (3) to give the defendants some confidence in seeing a black magistrate in court. Yet this respondent also considered that it was unlikely that working-class people, whom he would like to see on the Bench, would be appointed and, moreover, that 'middle-class blacks might react in the same way as middle-class whites'.

Many of those interviewees who wanted more black magistrates also expressed concern about the sort of people who would be likely to be appointed. There was opposition, for example, to any appointment that smacked of 'tokenism'; and the appointment of 'yes men' to the Bench was regarded as useless to the interests of the black communities. Another concern was that black appointees might be 'upwardly mobile, aspiring middle-class blacks' (Asian youth worker), as these were the sort of people who tended to be selected under the present system. Thus, according to one Asian law-centre worker, 'There should be more black J.P.s as long as the right people are chosen. The problem is how to ensure that.'

In some cases these doubts seem to have been sown or reinforced by the perceived performance of existing black magistrates. In Branston, for example, an Afro-Caribbean community worker described some of the black magistrates as being ready 'to sell the community out' and as 'living among us, but not being part of us'. In a similar vein a law-centre worker commented that they were 'too reluctant to be critical' in particular in not speaking out against stereotyping of Rastafarians in court. Perhaps the most trenchant criticism was directed against two black magistrates in Metropole County who had been on the Bench for a number of years and who were, we were told, out of touch with the grass-roots of the community. They were described as 'coconuts — brown outside and white inside!'

For a sizable minority of the black people to whom we spoke the appointment of more black people to the Bench, far from improving matters, was seen as a useless, even a retrograde step.

The people who expressed such views tended to be among those who were most critical of the way in which the local magistrates' court dispensed justice to black defendants. Yet they felt certain that having more black J.P.s would not alter this situation. They saw magistrates as having little scope for discretion. As the chairman of an Asian organisation stated, 'Magistrates cannot do much. They cannot alter charges; they cannot twist the law. You might end up with the irony of black magistrates enforcing a racist law.'

Another reason suggested to us in support of the view that the appointment of more black people would be ineffective was that, even if black magistrates start off with good intentions, 'they have to conform to the values of the institution' (chairman, Afro-Caribbean organisation) or, as one C.R.C. officer put it, they are likely to be 'swamped with establishment views'. Two of our respondents saw the situation in terms of social class rather than race. One, the chairman of an Afro-Caribbean organisation suggested that, '[the] issue of the magistracy is one of class, not colour. It is middle-class values being imposed on the local working-class community', while the other, a law-centre worker, stated that all magistrates adopted middle-class values whatever their race or background. 'Even if a black person is on the Bench, he takes a middle-class attitude, even if from a semi-skilled manual occupation.' This same interviewee went on to give a second reason why he saw the appointment of more black J.P.s as useless as a way of improving the quality of justice. 'By the time black kids get to court the damage is already done by lack of sympathetic legal counselling at the police station.' In his view more black solicitors and more black people on juries were more important reforms. A similar view was expressed by an Afro-Caribbean youth worker who pointed out that, 'Black magistrates won't be able to prevent the police from doing their tricks'.

It was also suggested by the ex-chairman of an Asian organisation that joining the Bench meant agreeing to impose alien values, 'becoming part of the state'. This, according to another interviewee might also render the black magistrate impotent in helping to bring about changes which would help his or her own community. 'There is a danger of some people who could help bring about change being lost to the community by becoming a J.P., because he or she is restricted in what they can do.' Thus the black magistrate ran the risk of becoming not only ineffectual in court, but equally ineffectual outside the courtroom. Such scepticism was taken still further by one Afro-Caribbean youth worker, who suggested that the appointment of black magistrates was merely a device to give the courts an acceptable appearance.

'They appoint black magistrates to save their own faces. They're taking black people to court and they find it helpful to have black people on the Bench. They use black people to legitimate what they do.'

Scepticism had been translated into action, or rather inaction, by four representatives of black community organisations we spoke to. They told us they had been approached to become candidates but refused. Although there were personal reasons which contributed to their decisions all of them refused in part because they were critical to a greater or lesser extent of the usefulness of black J.P.s to their communities. One of these interviewees echoed the argument that by becoming a J.P. he might risk becoming ineffective within the community. 'I see that some people once they get these positions they automatically turn. You know, they become indifferent to the community. They don't carry on as they used to carry on. There is a marked change in their attitude and I wouldn't like that to happen to me' (Chairman, Afro-Caribbean organisation). Another of those interviewed gave as one of the reasons he refused to become a candidate, that, 'People have a misconception about the power of magistrates. People will be disappointed if something goes wrong and you do not have the power to do anything about it' (Asian law-centre worker).

Yet these sorts of doubts and criticisms about the usefulness of black magistrates from within the black communities had not seemed to worry most black candidates for the Bench. Only a small minority of them had even considered these issues seriously. During our interviews with successful and unsuccessful black candidates, we had discussed whether they felt their joining the Bench had the support of their black community. For about 20 per cent this was simply not an issue; they tended to be candidates who had virtually no contact with their local black community. A majority of the candidates (about 55 per cent) seemed to assume automatically that their becoming a J.P. would have unanimous support within their black community. Only about a quarter seemed to be aware that there was criticism, within their own community, of black people joining the Bench. When it became known they had been appointed J.P.s several of this group in fact had been personally criticised. One Afro-Caribbean J.P. told us, 'I was accused of betrayal of my race,' and an Asian J.P. recalled being called, 'a traitor for being a magistrate'. Despite criticism directed at them personally, these two J.P.s and others who had similar experiences remained convinced that their being on the Bench was useful to their black community. Another Afro-Caribbean, a candidate for the Bench, argued the costs of joining the Bench were outweighed by the benefits. 'To a certain extent you will be used by the system, but if you make sure you get blacks a better deal, I'm talking about justice not law, then it's worthwhile.'

Critics of black people joining the Bench tended to be seen by black magistrates as being a relatively small proportion of their community. They were described for example as 'not very many' and as a 'vociferous minority'. According to one Afro-Caribbean J.P., some could be persuaded of the usefulness of black people joining the Bench. He told us, 'After I explained my motivation I got more support.' Another Afro-Caribbean J.P. told us he had been on the point of resigning and 'I only remained a J.P. because of the numbers of people who told me of the usefulness to the community of me remaining on the Bench'.

Part 4:

CONCLUSIONS

Chapter 14

SUMMARY OF RESEARCH RESULTS

THE APPOINTMENTS SYSTEM

1. Racial Prejudice and Discrimination

There is evidence of racial prejudice among some of the members of the Lord Chancellor's Advisory Committees and Sub-Committees. This takes the form of negatively stereotyping Asian and Afro-Caribbean people and applying such stereotypes in their expectations of black people's behaviour and in their assessment of their character and abilities (pp.60-1). Such attitudes could lead to direct and indirect discrimination (see pp.86-7) on the part of these selectors and administrators, even though such discrimination may not be deliberate (pp.88-90).

There is some evidence of direct racial discrimination and considerable evidence of indirect discrimination in the procedures adopted and the criteria applied by the selectors of magistrates. These included:

i. The deliberate exclusion in one area of some black and community relations organisations the failure to contact them as suitable community groups to put forward nominations for the magistracy, or to explain to them how the selection and appointment system works (pp.42-6).

ii. The emphasis, and in some areas almost exclusive dependence on, mainstream political parties and public service and middle-class charitable organisations as sources of recruits for the Bench (pp.43-4 and 94-5).

iii. The unofficial requirement in some areas that Asian candidates should be 'acceptable to the whole Asian community', while a similar requirement was not applied to white candidates (pp.71 and 89).

iv. The assumption by selectors in some areas that black candidates, particularly Pakistanis, are likely to owe more allegiance to their 'community' than to the pursuit of justice. This assumption results in black candidates being subject to confusing questions as to whether they see themselves as 'representatives' and, in some cases, in their rejection as a direct consequence of their replies to such questions. The selectors do not perceive white candidates in the same manner, unless the candidates belong to some specific body having policies which might affect the candidate's independence of judgement. In general, therefore, white candidates are not subjected to the same sort of questioning (pp.80-4 and 88-90).

v. The vague requirements of an adequate ability in written and spoken English and knowledge and experience of the 'English way of life', which are not applied equally to black and white candidates. Moreover, neither of these requirements are specifically related by the selection committees to the actual demands made of magistrates in their work on the Bench (pp.62-3 and 92-4).

vi. The emphasis in the selection process upon standards of performance during interviews conducted by formal panels with little appreciation among selectors of the disadvantages faced by some black candidates in such situations. There was no understanding among selectors of the particular problems experienced by black people when faced with a panel of all white interviewers (pp.95-6).

vii. The failure of the Lord Chancellor's Office in the thirty-five areas covered in our survey to ensure the appointment of any Afro-Caribbeans to Advisory Committees or Sub-Committees. Similarly the failure to appoint more than one person from the Indian sub-continent to act as a selector despite the fact that in some areas people of Indian and Pakistani origin account for 15-20 per cent of the population (pp.101-2).

viii. A failure by selectors to recognise the right and necessity for black people to engage in legitimate forms of public protest, such as demonstrations against what they perceive as discrimination and oppression. This results in those who participate in such protests being labelled as 'extremists' and 'controversial' by committee members and in their rejection as 'suitable' people for the magistracy' (pp.68-9).

2. Effects of Discrimination

The combined effect of such discrimination is difficult to estimate, but we suggest the following:

i. The rejection of black people who would, under a less prejudiced appointments process, have been selected for the Bench and who might have proved perfectly satisfactory magistrates.

136

Evidence for a high level of rejection of Asian candidates comes from three areas, where, in all, only seven out of forty-two applicants were accepted, a rejection rate of over 83 per cent compared to the figure for all candidates between 1981 and 1982 of about 73 per cent (pp.84-5).

ii. The selection of 'safe' black people whose attitudes may not reflect those of the majority of Asians and Afro-Caribbeans in the local communities towards issues habitually decided by magistrates' courts. Conversely the rejection of those who do reflect these attitudes and who may be highly regarded by these communities (pp.110-19 and 120-32).

iii. Discouragement to local black community organisations to put forward candidates and to indivudual black people to offer themselves for nomination. In some cases, it seems to have provoked disillusionment among black people with the selection system and with the magistrates' courts (pp.120-32).

3. Fairness

As regards its fairness to candidates in general, the system leaves much to be desired. In some areas secret enquiries are carried on behind the backs of candidates. The information obtained as a result of these enquiries is often second- or third-hand and is frequently no more than a single informant's highly subjective view of the candidate's abilities and character (pp.47-9). Candidates have no way of knowing what has been said about them, even though information obtained in this way may influence the decision of the selectors. No reasons are given to rejected candidates; in fact they are not even told that they have not been accepted.

4. Efficiency

Despite the confidence of officials in the efficiency of the selection process, we found it to be efficient in only two respects, its cheapness and its convenience for those responsible for its operation. In particular, we found that:

i. In some areas little or no efforts are made to increase the black communities' representation on the Bench despite the fact that the proportion of black magistrates is considerably below the incidence of black people in the local population (pp.39-42). In other areas the recruitment of black magistrates has been due almost entirely to the initiative of particular individuals and owes nothing to the policies of the Advisory Committee (p.45).

137

ii. The British tradition of the amateur is flourishing among those responsible for the selection of J.P.s They are amateurs in all senses of the term. First, Advisory Committee and Sub-Committee members are unpaid, people who perform their tasks out of a sense of public duty or because of the power which membership of these Committees carries. Secondly, neither the committee members nor the secretaries are appointed for their knowledge and skills in personnel selection. They receive no training whatsoever in this area. Most of those to whom we spoke seemed to regard choosing people to be magistrates simply as a matter of 'commonsense' and experience, for which no specialist knowledge or skills were necessary (chapters 6-8).

iii. With one or two exceptions, most local selection officials place too much emphasis on interview performance (ch.7). They display little knowledge of the process of person perception, the dynamics of the interview, or the skills needed in questioning candidates and assessing their abilities. The guidance offered by the Lord Chancellor's Department is of little or no help on these matters (pp.53-5).

5. Selection Criteria

i. The vagueness of the criteria of 'suitability' and the 'balancing of the Bench' both give plenty of scope for the personal biases and predelictions of selectors in the decision as to who should be appointed to the magistracy and who rejected (chs.8 and 10). The rule that those recommended to the Lord Chancellor should have the unanimous approval of all Advisory committee members places an effective veto in the hands of individual members (pp.28-34). To some degree political bias is avoided by the Lord Chancellor's insistance that all major political parties should be represented on these committees. However, there is nothing to prevent other forms of bias, such as racial prejudice from playing a part in the decision-making (ch.11).

ii. The lack of any firm criteria for selection combined with the fact that, once appointed, magistrates remain on the Bench until retirement age (unless guilty of serious misconduct) tends to make selectors extremely cautious and conservative in their choice of J.P.s (ch.8). We were particularly struck by the way some committee members and secretaries defined 'extremism' and by the way they regarded current minor motoring offences and current divorce proceedings as factors which disqualified, at least temporarily, some candidates from joining the Bench.

6. Role of the Secretary

The part played by the secretaries to the Advisory and Sub-

Committees has tended to be underestimated by official versions on how the system operates and by commentators on the system. We found that, particularly in those areas where the secretary doubled as Clerk to the Justices, he was an important figure, influencing both the policies and procedures of selection (p.34). We found that in one of our local study areas, the secretary was probably highly influential in the decision as to which candidates should be short-listed (p.49).

7. Numbers of Magistrates

i. The average number of sittings undertaken by magistrates in many areas was considerably above the minimum requirement of twenty-six per year. Some committees made it clear to candidates that they would be expected to exceed this average, which may have deterred some people from putting themselves forward or allowing their applications to proceed. In one area justices are required to sit every day for a week five or six times a year. Many working people cannot afford and/or cannot risk an arrangement of this sort (ch.9).

ii. The number of magistrates within the Commission areas covered by our survey was generally below and, in some cases, considerably below the establishment set by the Lord Chancellor's Office. Among those considerably below establishment are areas in which there is a significant black population. It is not therefore possible to explain the low level of black representation on the Bench in terms of shortages of places for new magistrates. In two areas, it was mentioned that some magistrates try to keep the recruitment figure low in order that they may spend more time in court (ch.9).

MAGISTRATES AND BLACK PEOPLE

The Black Magistrates

1. The number of black people coming forward as candidates for the magistracy is remarkably small, even in areas where there is a high Asian or Afro-Caribbean presence in the local population. The reasons for this lack of black candidates are complex, but may in part be related to features of the selection process and the failure of some Advisory Committees to seek out black people for the Bench (see 1(i), 2(iii), 4(i), and 7, above).

2. In twenty-three out of twenty-five of the areas covered in our

local research and survey of petty sessional divisions for which we were able to obtain accurate information, the proportion of black magistrates was such that it fell short of the proportion of black people in the local population (pp.101-2). In eighteen of these areas, even if the number of black magistrates were doubled, it would still not represent proportionately the local black population. There has, however, been a significant increase in the rate at which black people are appointed to the Bench. Over 60 per cent of the black magistrates identified in our survey were appointed since 1977 and over one-third became magistrates after 1980 (pp.99-100).

3. A much smaller proportion of black magistrates are women than in the magistracy as a whole. This lack of black women magistrates is particularly marked among Asian J.P.s of whom only 19 per cent were women compared with a national figure of 42 per cent (Cooke 1984) (pp.100-101).

4. Over 80 per cent of our sample of 190 black magistrates were engaged in non-manual work. 136 (71 per cent) of these came under Registrar General's Social Classes I and II (Higher Professional and Other Professional and Managerial. About 8 per cent were skilled manual workers and only 7 per cent worked in unskilled or semi-skilled jobs. These figures contrast strikingly with the available statistics for the proportion of manual workers within the black population which ranges between 59 and 69 per cent (pp.103-7).

5. All of the black magistrates we interviewed were or had at one time been very active in at least one area of local public life. About 60 per cent were involved in local politics (pp.107-110).

6. As might be expected, the black magistrates interviewed were generally strong advocates of the view that they were serving the interests of black people by being on the Bench. Few, however, saw their role in social or political terms, but they tended rather to regard their functions as black J.P.s as that of ambassador for black people and interpreter of the language and culture of their community for the benefit of defendants and other magistrates in court. A small number saw their role as including the prevention of racial discrimination by other magistrates (pp.110-19).

About 20 per cent of those black magistrates whom we interviewed were critical of the selection process. In the main, their criticisms were directed against the middle-class bias in the system and the relative dearth of black, particularly, black working-class magistrates (pp.114-6). Some also had harsh words to say about some of their white colleagues on the Bench, who, they said, tended to be racially prejudiced, out-of-touch with disadvantaged people and likely to believe the police on every occasion (p.118).

140

The Black Communities and the Magistracy

1. Complaints from black people about magistrates' courts were reported both by those Community Relations Councils who replied to our questionnaire and by the representatives of black community organisations whom we interviewed. Just under 80 per cent of the C.R.C.s who replied, stated that they had received complaints, but only ten of these mentioned that the complaints were frequent or very frequent. In certain areas, however, it was clear from the replies we received that feelings ran very high against alleged injustices and racial discrimination at the hands of the local magistrates. About half of the black community representatives had also received complaints about magistrates' courts (pp.120-4).

2. Specific complaints about the dearth of black magistrates were made by 20 per cent of the fifty-nine C.R.C.s returning our questionnaire. Yet, few of these indicated that there had been any local concern about the composition of the Bench (p.122). Representatives of black community organisations received few complaints on this score, but this cannot be taken as indicating general satisfaction among black sectors of the local community with the Bench's composition. Our interviews suggested that lack of interest in magistrates and their courts or ignorance of how the selection system worked, combined with the feeling that there was nothing useful black people could do to increase the number of black magistrates, were the real reasons behind the apparent acceptance of the present situation (pp.122-4). For similar reasons black community organisations tended to accord a low priority to the issue of black magistrates.

3. The majority of those representatives of black community organisations who knew something about the selection process tended to describe it in negative terms. They criticised the Advisory Committees for failing to contact their organisations and tended to see the process as one which almost automatically excludes working-class black people and anyone who speaks out against the police or injustice. In some cases the failure of candidates from these organisations to be appointed led to disillusionment and scepticism, and the organisation declining to put forward any more candidates (pp.124-7).

4. Two-thirds of our C.R.C. respondents were also dissatisfied with the selection system. The failure rate for candidates proposed by the C.R.C.s responding to our survey was as high as 84 per cent. As well as deploring the rejection of so many of their candidates, C.R.C.s were also dissatisfied with the secrecy of the system, its 'old-boy-network' style of operation and its discrimination against black people. The same disillusionment and scepticism which

characterised the attitude of some black organisations also affected a number of C.R.C.s. This was often directly attributable to past failures of black people whose candidature the C.R.C. had supported (pp.127-8).

5.The question whether an increase in the numbers of black magistrates would serve the interests of the black community received a wide range of responses from representatives of black community organisations. Some, like the majority of black magistrates, gave their wholehearted support to black people joining the Bench. Others, however, were opposed to the appointment of 'token blacks' and more middle-class black people whom they saw as identical to middle-class whites in their attitudes. A sizable minority regarded the appointment of black magistrates as a retrograde step for black people, as it legitimated the present social order and what they saw as discriminatory laws and law enforcement. They regarded those black people who had become magistrates as having 'betrayed their own kind' as having 'joined the other side' (pp.128-32).

6. Those black people who said that they were reluctant or unwilling to put themselves forward for the magistracy gave among their reasons:

   i. A general remoteness from the criminal justice system. A feeling that magistrates' courts are run by the white establishment and that black people would be out of place and unwelcome there (pp.120-8).

   ii. Lack of knowledge as to how one applies or is proposed for the Bench (pp.124-5).

   iii. The heavy demands on the time of some J.P.s, allied to fear of losing their job if they had to take time off to sit on the Bench or fear of losing promotion opportunities.

   iv. Too busy with community work to find the time to attend court as often as is required of magistrates locally (pp.75-6).

   v. Fear that they would lose their freedom of speech and action if they became magistrates. A recognition that there are restrictions on what magistrates may say and do in public and a belief that these would diminish their value to their own community (pp.130-1).

   vi. A view of black magistrates as 'tokens' or 'yes men' who do their community no good at all (pp.125-6 and 129-31).

   vii. The knowledge that in the past black people of high standing in the local community had failed to be appointed (pp.126-8).

Chapter 15

COMMENT

THE ARTICLES OF FAITH CONCERNING THE MAGISTRACY

Anyone putting forward criticisms with a view to reforming aspects of the lay magistracy faces serious problems, for in recent years the magistracy appears to have achieved a sacred status in British society similar to that of the monarchy, the House of Lords or, until recently, the police. Criticise it and one runs the risk of provoking a fierce defensive reaction from all those involved in operating the system, from Justices' clerks to government ministers. Perhaps in the past too many criticisms directed against the magistracy have tended to be uninformed and misplaced, but even those that have seemed to make good sense have frequently been met with high-handed assertions, total disdain or attempts to discredit the critics.

The response of Sir Thomas Skyrme, former Secretary to the Commissions, to the often-voiced criticism that the names of members of A.C.s should be made public, is typical. In his book, *The Changing Face of the Magistracy* (1979), he defends the anonymity rule by claiming that it protects A.C. members from being lobbied and that disclosure would lead to 'dissatisfaction among sections of the community who were not represented'. Both these arguments, he maintains, are based on experience, but he gives no information on how or when such experience was gained. Yet, in a reply to a Parliamentary Question (see Tate, 1983) the Attorney-General stated that those committees who had 'gone public' had 'experienced no comments or effects, adverse or otherwise'.

At about the same time that Skyrme's book was published, Elizabeth Burney's highly critical and well-researched study on the appointments system and the composition of local Benches also appeared (see Burney, 1979). While Skyrme's book received a long, detailed and laudatory review in *The Magistrate,* the organ of the Magistrates' Association, Burney's was merely listed as a 'publication received' and her research findings were not even mentioned in the pages of the journal.

Our final example concerns one of the authors of this report who, in 1981, sent the draft of an article he had written to a junior member of the Lord Chancellor's Department for comment before submitting it for publication. Sir Bryan Roberts, Skyrme's successor as Secretary of Commissions, responded by writing a letter to the author of the article accusing him of ignorance, prejudice, tendentiousness and irresponsibility.

At least this response was more than was achieved by the BBC *Checkpoint* team whose request for a formal interview and written answers to questions was simply refused.[48]

Our relations as researchers, however, with those members of the Lord Chancellor's Department at present responsible for the magistracy have been most cordial and the attitude of these officials towards the project, helpful and encouraging. But during the course of our discussions with them and our subsequent research, it became increasingly apparent to us that many of their policies concerning the appointment of magistrates are based upon articles of faith, illusions for which there is little, if any supporting evidence or attempt to obtain such evidence. It would appear that the peculiar position of the Lord Chancellor's Department of having no accountable minister in the House of Commons and no Select Committee to examine its policies and performance has protected it over the years from any serious public scrutiny and has facilitated the development of such articles of faith about the lay magistracy and the appointment process. These articles serve the dual purpose of guiding and sustaining present policies and those who operate them, and of providing ready-made answers to those who question these policies. Thus, the usual official reply to allegations of class imbalance on the Bench is the assertion that 'magistrates are drawn from all walks of life and all sectors of the community', instead of publishing the annual statistical returns from A.C.s, which would undoubtedly show a strong bias in favour of professional and managerial classes on almost all Benches.

Throughout our study of black magistrates we encountered these 'articles of faith' from the lips of many of the selection officials and J.P.s to whom we spoke. Where the system manifestly failed to live up to the ideals which these myths demanded, as, for example, where the proportion of black magistrates came nowhere near to reflecting the number of black people in the local population the official response was not to examine critically the selection process, but to assert that there were too few black candidates presenting themselves and that many of those who came forward were 'unsuitable'. Before we could tackle directly the social policy issues of race relations and justice, we realised that it was necessary to scrutinise and expose the assumptions behind those illusions. We recognised the need to contrast official assertions with what was actually happening within the selection system if we were going to make any progress at all towards formulating improvements to the present system which would eliminate or, at least, reduce discrimination and give black candidates a fair chance of becoming magistrates.

Article 1: The magistrates' task is to make 'the right decision' or to impose 'the proper sentence'

We discussed this proposition in some detail in the second chapter of our report. As we stated, it assumes that there are right and wrong decisions and that the way to such decisions is through the rational process of applying rules to facts. However, this type of decision-making rarely occurs in magistrates' courts. Most decisions involve the use of discretion, and the way discretion is exercised brings into play the values and beliefs of the decision-makers. The exposure of this assumption is fundamental to any assessment of the selection system, for a system based upon this myth of objective, de-personalised justice is able to ignore the class, racial or cultural backgrounds of the decision-makers, while emphasising that they should be 'well-balanced' people, endowed with 'commonsense' and 'the right motives'. In fact, as we have seen, the existing system does not ignore these factors entirely, but sees them as important only in order to give the Bench an acceptable face. Black people are thus appointed, not because of their values and beliefs, but because of some vague notion that the Bench should reflect the local community. Similarly, the exercise of 'balancing the Bench' is not done to ensure a wide spectrum of attitudes towards the sorts of questions which are decided by magistrates' courts but rather to prevent the magistracy from being dominated by any one political party or occupational group, and so avoid critical comments from politicians or from the press.

In fact this central notion of judicial decision-making by logical inference and careful balancing of the evidence holds true for only a handful of cases in magistrates' courts — cases in which inconsistencies in the evidence or logical improbability decide the issue. In the vast majority of cases decisions depend upon other factors. These include (1) the advice of the Clerk on issues of law and the application of the law to facts, etc.; (2) local Bench policy in sentencing, legal aid and the level of maintenance awards; (3) the values and beliefs of the magistrates in determining, for example, which witnesses are telling the truth, whether the defendant should be helped or punished or whether he or she is likely to commit further offences, and in deciding which parent should have custody of a child or whether a child will be abused if returned home. The values and beliefs relevant to this last set of factors are impossible to determine in advance. They depend upon the personality, cultural background, religion, education and prior experience of the decision-makers. These values and beliefs may be influenced by other members of the Bench hearing the case and also by the individual magistrate's conception of his or her role as a J.P.. To ignore the existence of these factors because they are difficult to pin down is like denying the therapeutic effect of some medicine because one does not know precisely how it works. Yet, this is exactly what those responsible for the selection of magistrates do in adhering to the article of faith of objective, depersonalised justice.

Article 2: The present selection system provides an effective method of determining which candidates are 'suitable' and which 'unsuitable' to be magistrates

The same pragmatic, rather simplistic, view of decision-making which characterises the official version of the magistrates' courtroom role also pervades the selection process. Judgements about people's future behaviour can, according to this set of beliefs, successfully be made through a cursory assessment of their personality, skills and intelligence. Allied to this view is a model of humanity which sees people as divisible into separate categories, those who have the immediate ability or potential to make 'good magistrates' and those who are so 'unbalanced' or 'extreme' in their opinions or behaviour, or so lacking in the necessary judgement, that they will never be suitable for the Bench. Of course, the very nature of the selection process forces selectors into categorising candidates, but what distinguishes the ethos of A.C.s and S.C.s from that of many other personnel selectors is that, far from accepting the artificiality of the categories and the subjectivity and limitations of attempts to push people into ready-made slots, it ascribes to the process an efficacy which is clearly misplaced, and attributes the selectors with powers which verge, according to some spokesmen for the system, upon the mystical or superhuman. S.C. secretary, 'You spot them through experience'; S.C. chairman, 'The gut reaction'. This belief in person-perception as a simple, straightforward, reliable process, and this confidence in the skills of untrained selectors to assess personality and character, contrast sharply with models of person perception and decision-making produced by psychology and the social sciences. These depict human behaviour as 'constrained — even determined — by identifiable forces lying outside their immediate control.

Psychology describes human skills and their limits' (Irving, 1984). Any doubts that the selectors had about the selection process were overcome by their belief that it actually worked.

Quite apart from the almost boundless opportunities for prejudice and discrimination offered by the vague selection criteria and the subjectivity of the process, the central notion that a candidate who cannot handle a formal panel interview necessarily lacks the skills and qualities required of a magistrate appears never to have been questioned by most of those responsible for operating the present system. Only one of the selectors to whom we spoke mentioned a committee recommending a candidate in spite of his interview performance; for the others the interview was everything or almost everything. There was little, if any, consciousness of the interview as a particular social situation, affecting different candidates in different ways, depending upon the class, cultural and racial background of both interviewers and candidates. Moreover, very little effort had been made to analyse in any systematic manner the specific skills and qualities required of magistrates and the possibilities and limitations of testing these skills and qualities reliably during the selection process, either during the interview or by some other method. What we have now is a system of selection 'on the cheap' which, understandably, limits the demands made on part-time, unpaid and untrained interviewers. It is a system which is sustained by a misplaced belief that because it seems to work there is no need to expose it to any critical examination.

Article 3: A Balanced Bench

The idea of a balanced Bench is superficially attractive both to selection officials and to those who criticise the selection system. Yet, not only is it an article of faith which promises much more than it is able to achieve, but, as we have seen, it also serves to provide ample opportunity for the exercise of unrestrained discretionary power by the Lord Chancellor and his advisers. Let us be absolutely clear. The exercise of balancing the Bench does not, as Skyrme would have people believe, 'make sure that each Bench is a microcosm of the local community' [Skyrme, p.62]. The arbitrary choice of categories for balancing purposes and the inevitable overlap of sex, occupational class, age and race make balancing Benches a highly subjective undertaking in which certain personal attributes are emphasised, while others are ignored completely. It may indeed help to facilitate the appointment of Labour supporters, those in manual jobs, and black candidates, and so prevent Benches in some areas being totally dominated by white, middle-class Tories; but it may also, at the same time, block the appointment of, say, young teachers or college lecturers who come from working-class families.

Moreover, the effect of balancing on the quality of justice, on the fairness of decisions, and on the extent to which they reflect the balance of opinion in the local community, is severely limited for two reasons. In the first place, the fact that there are, for example, some working-class or black J.P.s on the Bench of a petty sessional division does not mean that a working-class, black defendant is likely to appear before a bench of magistrates which will include someone from a similar class and racial background as himself, for all Benches have an overwhelming majority of white middle-class magistrates. Assuming, therefore, that there are three magistrates sitting in each courtroom, our research results suggest that the chances of a black defendant appearing before a black magistrate in areas where there is a sizable black community range between 3 and 21 per cent. If we take the petty session with the highest proportion of black magistrates, a defendant will have to appear on average five times before he or she sees a black face among the three magistrates hearing his or her case. Even if the black representation on the Bench actually reflected the average for the proportion of black people in the 20 P.S.D.s in Figure 4 (p.102), i.e. 6.2 per cent, the number of times would increase to 5.4 before a defendant saw a black face in front of him or her.

Applying our own research findings on the class distribution of black magistrates (pp.103-7), the chances that this one black J.P. would be a manual worker work out at about one in seven. For defendants who decide to contest the case against them, the odds against a working-class magistrate hearing the case are probably far higher, since few manual workers are able to take one or more full days off work to sit in courts. Such statistics of course, take no account of the possible influence of black J.P.s on the general attitudes and beliefs of other members of the Bench. This influence may well have some indirect effect on decision-making in individual cases. However, as we have already pointed out, there is no attempt by A.C.s to balance the Bench to achieve a spread of opinions on the sort of issues which come before the magistrates for determination. There is nothing, for example, to prevent members of A.C.s, and S.C.s who are more often than not themselves local magistrates, from preferring a black, working-class person who holds similar views to their own on issues of law enforcement or police evidence.

It should not be thought that we are arguing here against the general principle of appointing more black magistrates. Such appointees may, as we have seen, be able to counter or inhibit expressions of racism among other members of the Bench and increase knowledge about Asian and Afro-Caribbean attitudes and behaviour. They may also provide confidence-inspiring examples to other members of their community. What is important, however, is not so much the number of black faces on the Bench as the sort of people they are. Five black magistrates, who really have their roots among local Asians or Afro-Caribbeans, and who reflect the range of attitudes and beliefs existing within the black communities, may be far more influential in changing the way in which white magistrates perceive black people and their encounters with the law than ten black magistrates, who move almost exclusively in white circles and who have little contact with ordinary Asians or Afro-Caribbeans, people in other words whose attitudes and beliefs are likely to be no different from their white colleagues on the Bench.

POPULAR JUSTICE AND PROFESSIONALISM

Unfortunately, reform of the system for selecting lay magistrates is not simply a matter of dispelling a few myths. If this were so, such a secret, undemocratic process based upon patronage and word of mouth could not have survived so long into the second half of the 20th century. At the heart of this resistance to change lies a fundamental ambivalence about the role of the magistrate. This ambivalence has allowed those who maintain the present system to use two concepts of the lay magistracy which are essentially contradictory — that of the 'popular justice' and that of the 'professional'. These two concepts have become so confused that even would-be reformers become bemused about the sort of people magistrates should be and the sort of changes that should be introduced.

The 'popular justice' view emphasises the role of the Bench as representatives of the local community (see Pearson, 1981). Magistrates in any one area, it is thought, should reflect that community in terms of its class, race and political make-up. In its purist form it sees magistrates' Benches as much the same as juries, that is, representing the ordinary people, the community, in the justice system. People who appear before the courts, according to this view, should, as far as possible be judged by their peers, those from similar backgrounds as themselves, rather than by those with very different cultures and different values who have little or no understanding or appreciation of their way of life. Critics of the system who hold this view tend to draw attention to the class and racial bias of the Bench membership and to call for reforms which would ensure a wider social spread among recruits to the magistracy and, in particular, for many more magistrates who come from the same kinds of background as those who appear before the courts. However, this approach to the magistracy tends to ignore the fact that magistrates, unlike juries, are charged with a number of tasks which require training, experience and expertise. These include choosing a sentence among an ever-increasing and ever more complex list of possibilities, issuing warrants for search and arrest, determining conditions of bail and, in the case of magistrates in domestic and juvenile courts, deciding delicate issues of child custody, access and the placement of children in care.

The other view places much more weight on the 'professional' tasks and on the qualities necessary for someone who has the responsibility of performing them. Apart from the obvious lack of legal knowledge, a good magistrate, according to this view, should be like a good professional judge. He or she should possess those skills required for weighing up the evidence in a systematic and fair way in his or her decision-making and a detached professionalism in the manner in which he or she exercises their powers. Those who take this view tend to emphasise the importance of training and of recruiting people who have the potential to benefit from such training. The ones among them who take a critical stance point to the woeful inadequacy of existing training programmes in preparing justices for their decision-making role and to the inconsistency, bias and irrationality in the decisions of some magistrates.

Related to the concepts of popular justice and professionalism is the question of the magistrates' function as fact-finder and the view taken by many magistrates that their role should be that of protecting the existing social order. How can a person be expected to take an impartial view in a case involving contested police evidence, when that same person sees him or herself as having the responsibility of maintaining law and order, and supporting the police? A magistracy recruited like a jury for a limited duration, and having similarly limited fact-finding functions, would not be so prone as existing justices to identify with the criminal justice system and its crime-control responsibilities. People who join the judiciary, however they are selected, tend to become 'case-hardened' if they sit on the Bench repeatedly over a number of years, even if they do not start off identifying with the police, being sceptical of defendants' evidence and seeing themselves as personally responsible for public morality. They may find it difficult to ignore these responsibilities when they exercise their fact-finding role in contested cases, bail or detention.

Matters are not, of course, quite as simple as that. There are in the community many people who are even more supportive of the police than the most case-hardened magistrates, so that 'popular justice' would not necessarily mean fairer justice for the defendant in every case. Conversely a good 'professional' judge may be able to fulfil the fact-finding role throughout his or her career with unquestionable fairness to all and without cynicism or personal identification with forces of law and order. The skills and detachment and self-awareness associated with professionalism, therefore, do not necessarily mean unfairness to defendants. Now, it could well be argued that the trouble with the existing magistracy is that it offers the worst of both worlds — with 'ordinary people' chosen in part for their acceptance of and implicit wish to protect the existing social order; a training programme and controls over the quality of justice which fall far short of those necessary to ensure that magistrates exercise their functions in a truly 'professional' way; and a tenure of office which is limited only by the age of the incumbent and could last over twenty years. Yet this mixture of community representation and amateurishness often provides those responsible for operating the present system of lay magistrates with ready answers to its critics. Those who complain of the under-representation of some sectors of the community on the Bench and thus a breach of the ideal of popular justice can expect to be told that magistrates must be 'suitable' to exercise their many and varied judicial powers and responsibilities and that some sectors of the community do not offer a sufficient number of 'suitable' candidates to allow the selectors to fulfil the 'popular justice' ideal. Others, who criticise the quality of justice in the exercise of these powers can expect to be told that you cannot demand professional standards from unpaid part-timers who reflect the local community's interests. In other words the defects of the present system of selection have miraculously become virtues, or at least excuses for leaving things very much as they are. Similarly, what may appear to be incompatible concepts within the lay magistracy — those of 'popular justice' and 'professionalism' — are, through the subjective imposition of such filters as 'suitability' and 'balance' in the selection process combined, and the corps of justices that emerges, held up to the world as a fine example of the participation of a representative body of 'ordinary people' within an efficient legal system (see Hailsham, 1984).

The only way to provide a legal system which successfully combines 'professionalism' and 'popular justice' is to separate the function of fact-finding from the exercise of discretionary judicial power, as occurs in jury trials. Some commentators have indeed proposed reforms of this sort for magistrates' courts. They have suggested limiting the magistrates' tenure of office to five years or introducing 'mini-juries' for contested cases or elevating the role and status of the Justices' clerk from an adviser on questions of law to that of decision-maker on discretionary matters which involve interpretations of the law. Such proposals for radical change are, however, outside the scope of this report and for the purposes of our recommendations concerning the selection system, we have to acknowledge that the present organisation and role of lay magistrates within the legal system are unlikely to change within the foreseeable future.

Yet in our search for reforms that would help black people have a say in the exercise of judicial power, we have been unable to avoid entirely the dilemma posed by the issues of 'popular justice' and 'professionalism'. We wanted the selection process specificially to test the skills required of legal decision-makers and so eliminate as far as possible the vague and discretionary criteria it employs at present. However, we realised that to do this would do little for the cause of black people wishing to becoming magistrates. Indeed, it might even result in fewer of them being appointed, as black people may, on average, have had less opportunity to obtain the necessary education and experience to enable them to acquire magisterial skills.

One way to counter this problem within the selection system would be to introduce quotas to ensure that a certain number of places was reserved for members of black communities in accordance with their presence in the local population, even if this meant a lowering of the standard of skills required. This would resemble the positive discrimination popular in the United States during the 1970s. Yet, as a method of promoting black people to the Bench we found it unacceptable for two reasons. In the first place, our concern was not so much with numbers as with the type of black people who become magistrates, since, given the virtual impossibility for black people of achieving 'community justice', that is judgement by one's peers, (p.148) what is important is to ensure that those people who are really part of the black communities and who are therefore able to reflect the feelings and attitudes of its members have the opportunity to become magistrates. In other words, our principal concern was to prevent selection being confined to those black people who are acceptable to existing white magistrates. Our second concern was that any system of selection which lowered standards to accommodate black people would probably be unpopular among both blacks and whites. It would also run the risk of damaging the reputation of black magistrates, who might be considered to be less capable of doing justice than their white colleagues, because of the lower standard of qualification.

To overcome the dilemma posed by the incompatibility of 'popular justice' and 'professionalism' we have tried to devise a system which would allow more magistrates to develop the qualities associated with professionalism, (such as the ability to recognise when one's own preconceptions are influencing one's judgement, and a personal knowledge of the regimes and philosophies operating in different institutions for adult and juvenile offenders), while at the same time giving access to the Bench to people with a broad cross-section of attitudes and beliefs on those issues dealt with habitually by the courts. It is a system that would not disqualify people because their views were considered 'unsuitable' by committees consisting largely of existing magistrates. What we propose, therefore, is a two-stage selection process with a greatly improved training programme playing a central role, both in terms of its overall importance and its position between the two stages of selection.

Chapter 16

RECOMMENDATIONS

OUTLINE FOR A NEW SELECTION PROCESS

We have based our proposals for a new selection process on the civil liberty principles which we set out in the opening chapter of this report, and on the failures and short-comings of the present system as uncovered in our research. For reasons which will become apparent they emphasise the 'professional', as opposed to 'popular justice', view of the magistracy defined and discussed above. Figure 7 illustrates the main features of the proposed selection system. It will be seen that we have decided to retain the existing structure (see Figure 6) and some of the present arrangements, such as the Lord Chancellor's overall control and the role played by local A.C.s and S.C.s in recommending candidates. We accept that the work of finding and selecting candidates should be done at a local level and also that a central government department should have overall responsibility for the selection system and ultimate power to accept or reject the A.C.'s recommendations. We do not, however, regard this arrangement as ideal. In particular, we have strong reservations about the absence of any direct accountability of the Lord Chancellor's Department to the House of Commons or to any Select Committee of that House. Although the structure may appear similar to that which exists at present, this appearance is deceptive, as we envisage fundamental changes at each stage in the selection process and major reforms of the selection committees. Let us first deal with these committees.

Selection Committees

We propose that the membership of A.C.s and S.C.s should be, and be seen to be, completely independent of the local magistracy. While we accept that those who appoint magistrates should know something about the tasks which sitting on the Bench involves, we can find no justification for a system in which magistrates virtually appoint their successors and so have the power to perpetuate their own attitudes and beliefs both about justice and about those who are capable of doing justice as J.P.s. Furthermore, we can see little merit in retaining the concept of political balance on selection

Figure 6   Existing selection and training procedures

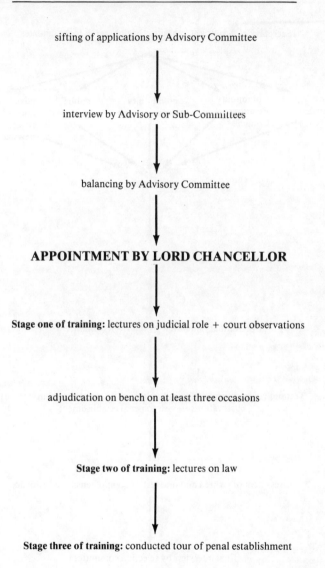

sifting of applications by Advisory Committee

interview by Advisory or Sub-Committees

balancing by Advisory Committee

APPOINTMENT BY LORD CHANCELLOR

Stage one of training: lectures on judicial role + court observations

adjudication on bench on at least three occasions

Stage two of training: lectures on law

Stage three of training: conducted tour of penal establishment

Figure 7 Proposed selection and training procedure

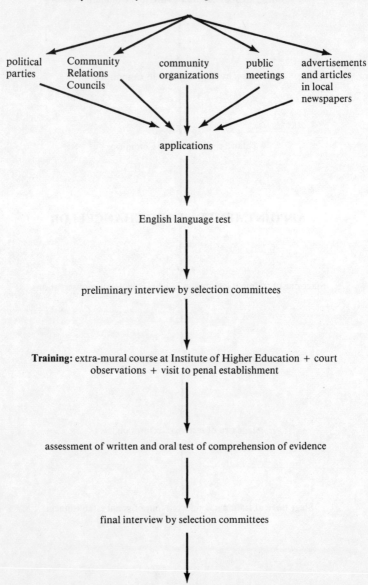

Secretary of Advisory Committee begins search for candidates

political parties   Community Relations Councils   community organizations   public meetings   advertisements and articles in local newspapers

applications

English language test

preliminary interview by selection committees

Training: extra-mural course at Institute of Higher Education + court observations + visit to penal establishment

assessment of written and oral test of comprehension of evidence

final interview by selection committees

APPOINTMENT BY LORD CHANCELLOR

committees, except as an expedient to avoid complaints of bias from one or other of the political parties.

Applying the principle of 'professionalism' which we elucidated earlier, we would choose as members of A.C.s and S.C.s people who had a particular contribution to make to the process of finding and selecting magistrates from all sectors of the local community. These would be:

1. People who know about magistrates' courts, including a probation office, a solicitor who undertakes defence work, a police officer, and a magistrate from a different Commission area or Sub-Committee area.[49]

2. People who know about the local community. This would include representatives from different ages, classes and ethnic groups in the area. In areas with large racial minorities, it might also include a member of the Community Relations Council. Similarly, in areas with youth unemployment problems, it could include a youth worker.

3. People who know about selection techniques. This would include members of the Institute of Personnel Management or others who had qualifications and/or experience in job selection.

The Lord Chancellor would continue to be responsible for the appointment of A.C. and S.C. members, but his insistence on people who are active members of mainstream political parties would cease. Instead of trying to obtain a political balance on committees, he would be responsible for achieving balance among the court representatives and among the community representatives. For the court representatives the balance should be between attitudes to crime and justice. Thus, the appointment of a police officer would be offset by the appointment of a defence lawyer or a probation officer. Similarly, community representatives would be balanced in terms of age, race and class and not simply for their political affiliations.

A typical A.C. in an area with a significant black minority among the population might consist of:

A magistrate (from a different area)
A solicitor specialising in defence work
A probation officer
A police officer
A Conservative councillor
An Afro-Caribbean youth worker
An Asian member of the Community Relations Council
A member of the Institute of Personnel Management.

It would be the responsibility of the Lord Chancellor's Department to find selection committee members. Provided that the notion of balance is respected, this could be done through advertising, or by formal requests to organisations such as the Law Society, the Association of Probation Officers or the Institute of Personnel Management. Appointments would be for three years only and the members of these committees would receive an annual stipend. Their names would be published in the local newspapers and would be available for public scrutiny at the public library and town hall. The official veto of A.C. members and effective, though unofficial veto, of S.C. members would be abolished. Instead there should be a rule stipulating that anyone recommended to the A.C. from the S.C. or from the A.C. to the Lord Chancellor should have received the support of at least two-thirds of the recommending committee. The chairperson of these committees should be elected each year by all committee members.

The Secretary to Selection Committees

We propose that the general policy in future should be for the secretaries of A.C.s and S.C.s to be appointed from among the qualified magistrates' court Clerks in the area. All appointees should undergo training in personnel selection either as part of the course for magistrates' Clerks run at present by Bristol, London and Manchester, or as a short training course. As a transitional measure, existing secretaries would be required to attend such a short training course. Once trained, they would be responsible for the selection procedures for the area. This would include actively seeking out candidates from those community groups which are reluctant to put forward names. They would not, however, be permitted to pre-select candidates.

Secretaries would be required to keep detailed statistics of all applicants to the magistracy, including their age, sex, occupation, political affiliation, race and religion. They would also be required to record the results of the candidate's interviews and selection tests, including the reasons given by selection committees for the candidate's rejection. The statistics and other information on each candidate and the result of his or her application would be filed each year at the Lord Chancellor's Office, which, in turn, would publish annual statistics on the selection of magistrates.

Intake

The objective of the A.C. secretary in seeking out candidates for the Bench would be to obtain as a broad a cross-section as possible, not only in regard to age, social class, geographical location and

158

political beliefs, but also in terms of values and attitudes concerning the kind of issues that are likely to present themselves in magistrates' courts. He or she should make a special effort to find candidates from those social groups who are unrepresented or under-represented on the Bench. The only organisations which would be excluded from this search would be those which by their public statements have made it clear that they are opposed to the principles of natural justice and the democratic process or which advocate racism or violence. Local organisations would not be excluded merely because the secretary or other members of the selection committee find them 'controversial' or 'extreme'. A list of all those local organisations approached and those excluded from the search for candidates should be made available for public scrutiny at the public library, town hall and magistrates' court.

All candidates would be required to submit a standard application form and provide the names of at least two referees. These referees would be sent a form to complete and return to the secretary. Discreet, behind-the-scenes enquiries would *not* be permitted, and any information obtained in this way or through unsolicited approaches by people who know the candidate would not be made available to the selection committee.

The Preliminary Interview

The purposes of this interview would be (a) to check that all the details on the application form were correct; (b) to ensure that the candidate would be eligible for appointment as a magistrate; (c) to ensure that the candidate understands the demands that will be made of him or her both during training and after appointment to the Bench and (d) to eliminate those candidates who clearly lack the capacity to undertake the training course or who demonstrate during the interview an unwillingness to respect the rules of natural justice, including a deliberate intention to be influenced in their decision-making on the Bench by matters extraneous to the facts of the case and the issues before the court. This would effectively prevent political or other organisations using the magistracy as a way of pursuing their policies and would exclude 'representative' candidates from the Bench while, at the same time, removing the ambiguity which at present eliminates some black candidates.

As far as the candidate's competence is concerned, this would be assessed by a simple test in written and oral comprehension. This test would be applied to all candidates and not just to those who have strong accents or who were not born or educated in this country.

The interview would be undertaken by three members of the selection committee, sitting with the secretary. The reasons for excluding any candidates at this stage would be recorded by the secretary.

Training

Without attempting to devise a whole new training scheme for magistrates, we believe that certain changes are essential if our proposed reforms to the selection system are to have any chance of success. Our 'professional' approach to the magistracy demands that no one should sit on the Bench without having been adequately trained for their duties. This principle was in fact recommended in the 1965 White Paper *The Training of Justices of the Peace in England and Wales,* but research carried out some seven years after its publication revealed that many new J.P.s were adjudicating in court without having completed even the first stage of their training programme (Baldwin, 1975). Although this situation may have improved to the extent that J.P.s now have to complete their first stage of training before sitting on the Bench, we would go further by proposing that no one should be *appointed* to the magistracy without having satisfied the A.C. that they had reached a required standard on the subjects covered by the course. Not only would this, we believe, improve the quality of justice in magistrates' courts, but it would also give an opportunity to less advantaged candidates to gain knowledge of the conventions of judicial behaviour and be exposed to ideas about punishment and social control through the law which might have been absent from their formal education or previous experience. In other words it could well avoid the present situation in which some people are disadvantaged in the selection process because of their ignorance of judicial conventions or lack of familiarity with certain implicit social theories about crime and punishment (see p.62). It would have the added advantage of ensuring that people who were not sufficiently motivated to treat the training seriously would not be appointed to the Bench, whereas, at present such people could be appointed before they are required to undertake any training.

We would also go further than the White Paper in the form and content of the lectures which aspiring magistrates would be required to attend. The White Paper proposed lectures on law and procedure which explained the

necessity for decorum on the Bench and stress what is meant by judicial attitude, a judicial mind and acting judicially . . . the relationship between the Bench and the Clerk and other staff will be explained and also the positions and functions of advocates and the police.

Under present arrangements the Training Committee of Magistrates' Courts Committees (administrative bodies on which magistrates and the local council are represented), are responsible for magistrates training. Some arrange for local institutions of higher education to put on a course of lectures as part of their extra-mural programme, while others put the training programme entirely in the hands of the Justices' clerk (Burney, p.199). We find this second arrangement amateurish and unsatisfactory. Although each year some Justices' clerks attend a course at Homerton College, Cambridge, on adult teaching techniques, their qualifications are as lawyers, not as educators. Their specialised training is in law and procedure and not in decision-making and communication skills,[50] yet their influence over the attitudes of new recruits to the Bench can be considerable.[51] Although it is true that some clerks do succeed in putting on interesting and imaginative courses with the help of visiting speakers, it is not very surprising that others, according to Burney 'get bogged down in [the] sticky fields of law and procedure' (p.206).

Burney also complains that there is not enough on the 'public relations' angle of the magistrate's role and that as a consequence magistrates often have difficulty in communicating with defendants and witnesses in court. Her view reinforces our own more general concern that far too little attention is paid in training to what might be called 'the informal aspects of magistrates' functions'. Our particular concern is that magistrates should be aware of the dynamics of group decision-making and the complex ways in which people perceive others and make decisions about their character, motivations and likely future behaviour. This would include making trainee magistrates aware, or heightening their awareness, of their own prejudices and values and how these might be held in check in decision-making. There is sufficient accessible literature now in this area to make it possible to incorporate training in these aspects of a magistrate's role without handing over the entire course to a team of psychologists. A useful comparison is to the training of panel members for Scottish children's panels which gives prominence to this important aspect of decision-making.

Courses should be under the immediate control of a course tutor from the higher education institution putting on the course and he or she should be responsible to the Magistrates' Court Committee, which would have the task of appointing the course tutor and allocating funds for lecturers and facilities. General responsibility for the training of magistrates should be with the Lord Chancellor. His Department should provide guidance for course tutors to ensure that all courses cover certain core subjects and should guarantee that standards of training are maintained at a consistent level throughout the country.

The Final Assessment

This would consist first of all of a test in oral and written comprehension. This could well take the form of candidates listening to a pre-recorded tape or watching a video recording of a simulated courtroom case, which might include technical legal terms as well as conflicts of fact and law. Candidates would then have to answer questions on what they had heard. The written test could take the form of a mock social enquiry report on which candidates would once more have to answer questions and to demonstrate in their answers that they had fully understood its contents.

The final interview, like the tests, would be concerned with ensuring that all those appointed to the magistracy had the necessary skills and knowledge to sit on the Bench. The interview panel would receive an attendance record for each candidate from the course tutor, together with the results of the comprehension tests. They might well present the candidates with hypothetical bail or sentencing problems to see whether they had absorbed the contents of the course lectures and were able to apply these in practice. There would, however, be no attempt to assess candidates' character or political opinions during the interview and the only reason for disqualifying candidates at this stage would be the failure to achieve the required standards in knowledge and skills necessary for the satisfactory performance of the functions of a magistrate. Any candidate whom the panel decided should not be recommended for appointment would be given the reasons for his or her rejection.

Since the A.C., and in particular, the secretary to that Committee, would have made a positive drive to solicit candidates from all sections of the local community at the start of the selection process, there would be no need for the A.C. to engage in what we consider to be a highly dubious balancing exercise (see ch.10). However, it would be the responsibility of the Lord Chancellor's Department to ensure that Benches were not monopolised by a particular political party, racial or religious group, or social class. In the annual returns to the Lord Chancellor's Department, the secretary of the A.C. would, therefore, include brief profiles of all candidates, successful and unsuccessful. These profiles of successful candidates would also be published in the local newspaper. The Lord Chancellor's officials would, where there was any risk of a Bench becoming socially unbalanced, advise the secretary to seek out applications from those social groups which were under-represented on the Bench. There would be no question of disqualifying or delaying the appointment of good candidates for reasons of balance.

There are, we admit, two major disadvantages with the scheme we propose. In the first place it will cost considerably more than the existing arrangements for the selection and training of magistrates. Given the improvements which we anticipate in the quality of justice, we believe that it will be money well spent. The second disadvantage lies in the fact that, without any guarantee of appointment, aspiring magistrates will have to attend a full training course and submit themselves to two interviews and assessments. All this may well have the effect of deterring some of those people who would otherwise have volunteered their services. As we have already suggested, this may be a good thing in the case of any who wish to be magistrates for reasons of power and status. However, there will probably be others who will be frightened away by the rigour of the new selection process and by the demands it makes on the time of candidates. Clearly motivation is an important factor in determining whether candidates are likely to make good magistrates, but if the number of candidates for the magistracy is not to fall dramatically and if the magistracy is not to continue to rely upon a middle-class concept of public service for its recruits, the job must be made more attractive to all sectors of the community. This would mean realistic payments for loss of earnings and, in many areas, a reduction in the number of sittings expected of J.P.s to a level approaching the Lord Chancellor's minimum requirement of twenty-six per year.

Changes in the Law

1. We propose that the Race Relations Act and Sex Discrimination Acts be amended to include clearly within their ambit appointments to the magistracy. We see no reason why these appointments should be immune from the scrutiny of the courts and tribunals. Indeed, such scrutiny would provide some much needed accountability for selectors and contribute to public confidence in the selection system. Moreover, the major problem at present in enforcing discrimination laws, that of evidence, would to some

degree be relieved by our proposals for lifting the secrecy of the system and giving to all unsuccessful candidates a note of the reasons for their rejection. It should also be assisted by the far more limited discretion available to selectors under the system we propose.

2. We recommend that the provisions in the Employment Protection (Consolidation) Act 1978 be strengthened to give employees a right to serve on the Bench for the required minimum twenty-six sessions a year. Any employers not prepared to agree to their employees' absence for this purpose should be able to apply for exemption to an Industrial Tribunal. The onus, in other words, should be on the employer rather than the employee as at present. The tribunal should be empowered to grant an exemption in exceptional cases or to award an annual sum by way of compensation to be paid to the employer.

The Lord Chancellor should press the Treasury for a special fund to be set up for the purpose of compensating employers who lose money as a result of essential employees taking time off to sit on the Bench. No doubt this will be expensive compared to the minute price paid at present for the lay magistracy. Yet to continue with the present reliance on the goodwill of employers is increasingly unrealistic in these time of economic stringency and fierce competition both for orders and jobs. Without such financial backing, becoming a magistrate is unlikely to prove an attractive proposition except for the comfortably off or those employed by public bodies. Whatever reforms are made in the actual selection process, the promise of a Bench which fulfils the ideal of reflecting all sectors of the community will never be realised as long as there are serious economic barriers standing in the way of those who do not have the privilege of financial security.

NOTES

PART I

1. See Kettle, 1982, Crow and Cove, 1984. See also Ferdi, 1983, for an account of the relation between the number of black defendants and of black probation officers.
2. For example, *The Law Machine* ITV (1983); *Judge Thy Neighbour — Brass Tacks Report* BBC2 (1983); *Checkpoint*, Radio 4 (1983).
3. See Hood, 1962; King, 1971; Levenson, 1982; and Tarling, 1979.
4. Tarling, 1979.
5. Peay, 1980 and 1981.
6. King, 1971; Zander, 1971; Levenson 1982.
7. See e.g., Floud and Young, 1981.
8. See Saks and Hastie, 1978, p.55.

PART II

9. Sir Thomas Skyrme's book, the only published source on this subject states:
    '. . . In April 1962, the Nottingham Committee submitted ⸍the name of Mr E.G. Irons, a West Indian engaged in welfare work, who then became the first immigrant magistrate. Since then seventy-eight other immigrants, mostly from the West Indies, India and Pakistan have been appointed to Benches throughout the country.' (Skyrme, 1979, p.62)
10. See eg., Willis, 1983, p.9.
11. Information contained in letter addressed to Michael King from Mr T.C. Spicer, Assistant Secretary of Commissions, dated 31 March, 1982. See also Cooke, 1984.
12. Letter from Major Peter Clarke, Secretary to the Duchy of Lancaster to Michael King, dated 16 April, 1982.
13. See note 11 above.
14. See note 11 above.
15. *Directions for Advisory Committees on Justices of the Peace,* para 8, p.2.
16. Information obtained orally from Mr T.C. Spicer, Assistant Secretary of Commissions.
17. See note 16.
18. *Directions for Advisory Committees on Justices of the Peace* (D.A.C.J.P.) is the main source of such guidance. This booklet was confidential, but a copy was sent to Michael King in May 1984 with a letter from Mr Brian Cooke, Secretary to the Commissions, stating that its confidential status had been revised.
19. Information contained in the Lord Chancellor's Office standard form

of *Particulars of a person to be considered for appointment as a Justice of the Peace* which is sent to candidates.

20. See note 19.
21. See note 19.
22. D.A.C.J.P. (note 19) para. 24.
23. This usual practice that we encountered was for the A.C. to rely upon S.C.s on the issue of the candidate's suitability while it dealt with the question of balance. Occasionally an S.C. would ask the A.C. to decide upon the suitability of a candidate where the S.C. could not itself reach agreement.
24. See Burney, 1979; Pearson, 1981.
25. Hood, 1973; Burney, 1979.
26. The complete list of organisations which the Lord Chancellor's Office sets out in para. 21 of the D.A.C.J.P. as being useful for the purpose of finding suitable candidates is as follows:

Athletic Clubs	Industrial and Commercial Firms
Clergy and Religious Organisations	Medical Practitioners
	Political Parties
Chambers of Trade or Commerce	Professional Organisations
	Teachers Organistions
Co-operative Societies	Trade and Labour Councils
Councils of Social Service	Trade Union Branches and Organisations
Employers Organisations	
Ex-Service Organisations	Women's Organisations
Friendly Societies	Working Men's Clubs

27. Harley was the one area in our local study which advertised for candidates in an Urdu language paper.
28. There were exceptions. The most active 'political sponsor' of black candidates in Branston was a prominent member of the Liberal Party who readily supported the applications of black people whatever their political affiliations. In Harley one of the Asian candidates was 'sponsored' by the local Conservative party agent.
29. See eg: King, 1981, pp.92-5.
30. The establishment is calculated by taking the total number of Bench sittings per year and dividing this figure by the number of justices and the average workload of the Bench. The Lord Chancellor's Office checks the establishment each year. The objective of this calculation is to ascertain how many justices are required to cover all the sittings of a Bench so as to produce an acceptable average attendance figure for the Bench.
31. The Establishment figures for the five areas of our local study together with the actual number of active J.P.s on the Bench are set out below.

	No. of active J.P.s in P.S.D.	Establishment
Branston	225	300
Harley	223	240
Meadowport	239	300
Metropole County	729	890
Thorburn	171	200

32. Justices' Allowances Regulations, 1979, as applied by Home Office Circular No.85 'Financial Loss Allowance'. These amounts are payable only where the magistrate can prove actual loss of earnings or income — a rule which may well prevent self-employed people from claiming any allowance. When paid, the allowance is tax free.
33. See Runnymede Trust, 1983.
34. See Baldwin, 1976; Hood, 1972; Burney, 1979.
35. Burney (1979) gives a graphic account of this struggle in Chapter 3.
36. There were in fact four Moslems on the Bench at the time. The interviewer discovered a fourth after this interview had taken place.
37. *Knight* v. *Att. Gen., and Anor.* (E.A.T.) I.C.R. [1979] pp.194-201.
38. *Bohon-Mitchell* v. *Common Professional Examination Board* [1978] I.R.L.R. p.252.
39. *Ojutiky and Oburoni* v. *Manpower Services Commission* [1982] I.R.L.R. p.422.
40. *Bohon-Mitchell* (see note 38).
41. See note 33.
42. A study of local politics in Birmingham in the late 1960s and early 1970s concluded that because they were organised around class divisions, political parties made little or no effort to attract black people. It was argued also that black people for their part, found the parties 'difficult to approach and, some would argue, not even worth the effort of trying'. Newton, 1976, p.216.

PART III

43. See Gregory, 1976. See also James Report, pp.143-6.
44. See note 43.
45. See note 43.
46. Nine C.R.C.s (15.3 per cent) did not respond to this question.
47. Six C.R.C.s (10 per cent) did not respond to this question.
48. Tate, 1983.

PART IV

49. Such a system already operates in Metropole County where S.C. members do not select magistrates for the P.S.D.s where they sit on the Bench.
50. The basic syllabus for training magistrates is contained in the Lord Chancellor's Department's Handbooks.
51. See Astor, 1984, pp.359-389; Bond and Lemon, 1979.

BIBLIOGRAPHY

Allport, G. and Postman, L. (1947) *The Psychology of Rumour,* Holt, Rinehart & Winston, New York.

Asch, S.E. (1946) 'Forming Impressions of Personality', *Journal of Abnormal and Social Psychology,* Vol.41, pp.258-90.

Astor, H. (1984) *'The Role of the Clerk in Magistrates' Courts,* unpublished Ph.D. thesis, Brunel University.

Baldwin, J. (1976) 'The Social Composition of the Magistracy', *British Journal of Criminology,* Vol.16, No.2, pp.171-74.

Bartlett, D. & Walker, J. (1973) 'Making Benches — The Inner Wheel', *New Society,* 19 April.

——— (1975) 'Wheel of Information'; *New Society* (25 December).

Bayne, R. (1977) 'Can Selection Interviews be Improved?', *Journal of Occupational Psychology,* Vol.50, No.3, pp.261-67.

Bond, R.A. and Lemon, N.F. (1979) 'Changes in Magistrates' Attitudes During the First Year on the Bench', in *Psychology, Law and Legal Processes,* Lloyd Bostock, S. (ed.), Macmillan, London.

Brigham, J. (1971) 'Ethnic Stereotypes' *Psychological Bulletin,* Vol.76, pp.15-38.

Burney, E. (1979) *J.P.: Magistrate, Court and Community,* Hutchinson, London.

Carlson, R., Thayer, D., Mayfield, E. and Peterson, D. (1971) 'Improvements in the Selection Interview', *Personnel Journal,* April.

Cooke, B. (1984) 'The Appointment of Justices of the Peace — The Advisory Committee System', *The Magistrate,* Vol.40, No.5.

Crow, I. and Cove, S. (1984) 'Ethnic Minorities and the Courts' *Criminal Law Review,* pp.413-17.

Farrington, D. and Morris, M. (1983 (i)) 'Do Magistrates Discriminate Against Men?' *Justice of the Peace,* 17 September.

——— (1983 (ii)) 'Sex, Sentencing and Re-conviction', *Brit. Journal of Criminology,* Vol.23, p.229.

Ferdi, D. (1983) 'The Trust Unit', *The Guardian,* 21 September.

Floud, J. and Young, Y. (1981) *Dangerousness and Criminal Justice,* Heinemann, London.

Gregory, J. (1976) *Crown Court or Magistrates' Court,* Report of the Social Survey Division of the Office of Population Censuses and Surveys, H.M.S.O. London.

Hailsham, Lord (1984) Speech at Annual General Meeting of Magistrates' Association, 12 October, unpublished.

Hood, R. (1962) *Sentencing in Magistrates' Courts,* Stevens, London.

——— (1972) *Sentencing the Motoring Offender,* Heinemann, London.

Irving, B.L., (1984) 'Psychology and Policing: Past and Present', *British Psychological Society Division and Legal Psychology,* Newsletter, April.

James, Lord Justice (ch) (1975) *Interdepartmental Report on the Distribution of Business between the Crown Court and the Magistrates'*

Courts, Cmnd. 6232, HMSO. London.

Kettle, M. (1982) 'The Racist Numbers Game in our Prisons', *New Society,* 30 September, pp.535-7.

King, M. (1971) *Bail or Custody,* The Cobden Trust, London.

———— (1981) *The Framework of Criminal Justice,* Croom Helm, London.

Levenson, H. (1982) 'Legal Aid League Tables', *Legal Action Group Bulletin,* February, pp.8-10.

Lord Chancellor's Department (1965), *The Training of Justices of the Peace in England and Wales,* Cmnd 2856. H.M.S.O., London.

Lustgarten, L. (1980) *Legal Control of Racial Discrimination,* Macmillan, London.

Newton, K. (1976) *Second City Politics: Democratic Processes and Decision-Making in Birmingham,* Clarendon Press, Oxford.

Peay, J. (1981) 'Mental Health Tribunals — Just or Efficacious Safeguard?', *Law & Human Behaviour,* Vol.5, pp.161-86.

———— (1980) *Mental Health Review Tribunals — a Study of Individual Approaches to Decision-Making.* Unpublished Ph.D. thesis, University of Birmingham.

Pearson, R. (1981) 'Popular Justice and the Magistracy: The Two Faces of Lay Participation'. in Z. Bankowski and G. Mungham (eds.) *Essays in Law and Society,* RKP, London.

Reading, T. (1977) 'How Interviews Fail', *Management Today,* April, pp.33-38.

Riboux, P. and Poppleton, S. (1978) *Psychology at Work: An Introduction,* Macmillan, London.

Rodger, A. (1975) 'Interviewing Techniques' in *Recruitment Handbook* (2nd edition), Ungerson, B. (ed.), Gower Press, Epping, Essex.

Royal Commission on *Justices of the Peace* (1948), Cmnd. 7463 H.M.S.O., London.

Royal Commission on *The Selection of Justices of the Peace* (1910), Cmnd. H.M.S.O., London.

Runnymede Trust (1983) 'Unemployment and Black People' *Race and Immigration,* No.159, pp.7-11.

Saks, M. and Hastie, R. (1978) *Social Psychology in Court,* Von Nostrand, Reinhold, New York.

Secord, P. and Backman, C. (1964) *Social Psychology,* McGraw Hill, New York.

Skyrme, T. (1979) *The Changing Face of the Magistracy,* Macmillan, London.

Tarling, R. (1979) *Sentencing Practice in Magistrates' Courts,* Home Office Research Study No.56, H.M.S.O., London.

Tate, T. (1983) 'Magistrates on Trial', *The Listener,* 15 September.

Vennard, J. (1982) *Contested Trials in Magistrates' Courts,* Home Office Research and Planning Unit, Report No.71, H.M.S.O., London.

Willis, C. (1983) *The Use, Effectiveness and Impact of Police Stop and Search Powers,* Home Office Research and Planning Unit Paper No.15, H.M.S.O., London.

Zander, M. (1971), 'A Study of Bail Decisions in London Magistrates' Courts', *Criminal Law Review,* p.195.

Appendices

APPENDIX I

Letter from Lord Chancellor's Department to Advisory Committee Secretaries

Lord Chancellor's Department
Neville House, Page Street
London SW1P 4LS

Your reference:
Our reference: JP 2/55/01

Telephone 01-211 0209
11th February 1983

Dear Sir,

Selection of Candidates for the Magistracy — Ethnic Minorities

A team from Warwick University is conducting research on this topic. The project is being financed by the Cobden Trust, a registered charity, which for the past twenty years has been supporting research and education work in the area of legal rights and responsibilities.

The purpose of the project is to ascertain the extent of, and to identify the factors which affect West Indian/African and Asian membership of magistrates' Benches. There are three objectives:

i. Identifying factors which affect the number of West Indians/Africans and Asians who are proposed to Advisory Committees as candidates for the Bench.

ii. Consideration of the procedures adopted by Advisory Committees in selecting suitable candidates to recommend to the Lord Chancellor, with particular reference to West Indian/African and Asian candidates.

iii. The collection of information about the extent of West Indian/African and Asian membership of magistrates' Benches and of Advisory Committees, and whether this has changed in recent years in areas in England and Wales where members of these communities are a significant proportion of the local population.

A survey will be conducted to collect information. Also more detailed research will be carried out in three or four areas.

The research will be conducted by Colin May, Research Fellow in the School of Law at Warwick University, who will be working on the project full-time. He will work under the direction of Michael King, lecturer in the same School of Law.

170

Proposing Organisation Individuals	No. of Candidates Proposed			No. of Candidates Appointed		
	W.I.	Asian	African	W.I.	Asian	African
a.						
b.						
c.						
d.						
e.						
f.						
g.						
h.						
i.						
j.						
k.						

(Please continue on a separate sheet if necessary)

The Number of West Indian, African and Asian Magistrates

10.(a) Has the number of West Indian, African and Asian Magistrates in your area in recent years shown: A large rise/A slight rise/No change/A slight fall/A large fall?

(b) Please give details.

11. Does your C.R.C. take the view that the present number of West Indian, African and Asian people who are members of the Bench in your area is: too high/about right/too low/much too low?

12.(a) Is your C.R.C. satisfied with the present procedures for selecting magistrates in your area? Yes/No (please circle).

(b) If no, please specify what you consider to be the difficulties with the present procedures and any improvements you would like to see.

Public Concern

13.(a) Has there been any public concern over West Indian, African and Asian membership of the Bench in your area? Yes/No (please circle).

(b) If yes, could you please let us have copies of any press cuttings, correspondence or other information. (Confidentiality will be respected. We will reminburse costs).

Magistrates' Justice

14.(a) Have you received any complaints from members of the West Indian, African or Asian communities about the attitudes of magistrates at your local courts? Yes/No (please circle).

(b) If yes, how often have you received complaints in the last three years? Very often/Often/Not often/Never.

(c) Please specify the main types of complaints made.

(d) How often has the composition of the magistrates' Bench been a matter of complaint? Very often/Often/Not often/Never.

Magistrates and Race Relations
15. Does your C.R.C. consider that having a representative proportion of magistrates from the local West Indian, African and Asian communities is:
Very important for good relations.
Quite important for good race relations.
Not very important for good race relations.
Irrelevant to good race relations.

16. Do you have any further comments you wish to make on matters raised in this questionnaire?

Thank you for your co-operation.

Colin May
Cobden Trust
21 Tabard Street, London SE1 4LA.

APPENDIX III

RESEARCHERS' INTERVIEW GUIDES

INTERVIEW GUIDE: REPRESENTATIVES OF ADVISORY COMMITTEES

1. Committee.

2. Name and Position.

A. Vacancies
I would like to ask you some questions about how vacancies are filled.

3.(a) How many vacancies do you have (each year) on average?

  (b) How is the no. of vacancies arrived at?

  (c) Do applications always exceed the number of vacancies? Yes/No.

4.(a) Are vacancies ever left unfilled? Yes/No.

  (b) If yes, how frequently?

  (c) Reasons for answer to (a)

5. The L.C. Dept. has told us of the emphasis upon 'balancing' the Bench. What does the committee understand by the concept of a 'balanced' Bench?

6. How does the committee set about achieving a balanced Bench? (What criteria? Race?)

7.(a) Does the committee ever decide it wants particular kinds of people (ie, particular age, sex, section of society)? Yes/No.

  (b) On what basis are such decisions made?

8.(a) Does the committee consider the procedure for applying for the magistracy is widely enough known by the 'general public'? Yes/No.

  (b) If no, has the committee ever taken active steps to publicise the procedure? Yes/No.

  (c) If yes to (b), what were they? When were they taken?

  (d) Was there any particular reason for (c)?

9.(a) Does the committee let it be known when there are vacancies on the Bench? Yes/No; Always/Sometimes/Never.

  (b) Reasons for Yes or No to (a).

  (c) If yes to (a) how?

10.(a) Are certain groups/organisations regularly notified of vacancies? Yes/No.

  (b) Has this always happened? Yes/No (dates).

  (c) Which groups/organisations?

  (d) Why these organisations?

B. Selection Process — General
I want to ask you some questions about what the committee looks for and its experience in selecting candidates for nomination from the applications received.

11. What personal qualities should a magistrate have?

12. Is it the committee's view that magistrates' decisions are similar to professional/admin. decisions, and therefore they should have abilities appropriate to prof. decision-makers, or are magistrates' decisions based more on instinct as to who is lying, therefore requiring different abilities?

13.(a) In the committee's experience, is it difficult to find people with the right qualities? Yes/No.

  (b) Please expand on (a).

14.(a) Is it more difficult to find West Indians etc. with the right qualities than white people? Yes/No.

  (b) Why do you think this is?

Initial Processing
Now I would like to ask in some detail about how the committee processes the applications it receives.

15.(a) What are the first steps that are taken once applications are received?

176

(b) What is the objective?

(c) Is all the Committee involved?

16. How useful to the committee is it if a member has some personal knowledge of the candidate?

17.(a) In your experience do committee members have personal knowledge of West Indian etc., candidates more or less frequently than white candidates?
More/Less/About the same.

(b) Expand — why do you think this is so?

18.(a) Are enquiries made about all candidates or only some? All/some.

(b) If only some, why?

19.(a) Do you make enquiries about the candidates before or after you decide who to select for interview?
Before/After.

(b) How long on average do the enquiries take?

(c) What sort of things do the enquiries cover? (probe different enquiries made about West Indians etc.?)

20.(a) Does making enquiries about West Indian etc., as against white candidates present any particular difficulties? Yes/No.

(b) If yes, Why?

21. How much weight do you give to the personal enquiries as against the form.

Interviewing

22. How many people are in the interview panel usually?

23.(a) Are they all advisory committee members? Yes/No.

(b) If no, who are the non-advisory committee members of the interview panel?

24. Where do the interviews usually take place?

25. What criteria are used for selection?

26. Does the panel decide in advance how the interview is to be organised, eg, are questions divided up in advance?

27.(a) Does the panel try to compare candidates in the interview situation? Yes/No.

(b) If yes, how?

(c) If no, are candidates asked the same questions? Yes/No (Why/Why not?)

28. In general, what are candidates asked about?

29. Is there anything it is considered especially important to cover if the candidate is West Indian, etc., rather than white?

30. Are the answers recorded in anyway? Yes/No.

31.(a) Does the panel ever have time to consider the interviewing technique it employs? Yes/No.

(b) If yes, please expand.

32. Is there any difference in the performance of West Indian etc., candidates in the interview in comparison with white candidates? Yes/No (What differences? Reasons for differences?)

33. What weight is given to interviewing in considering a West Indian etc., candidate in comparison with a white candidate?

Nomination

34.(a) Does the interview panel make a recommendation to the Advisory Committee. Yes/No.

(b) If yes, is the recommendation usually accepted without discussion? Yes/No.

(c) If no to (b) please expand.

35. If there is any disagreement about whether to recommend nominations, how is it resolved? (Vote, Veto, Chair's sense of the meeting?)

36. If suitable candidates exceed vacancies how does the committee select its nominations?

37.(a) Has the committee ever had nominations refused by the L.C. Dept? Yes/No.

(b) If yes, how frequently?

(c) If yes, has this affected the committees subsequent nominations?

38.(a) We understand it is policy not to inform candidates who are not recommended of the outcome? Yes/No.

(b) Why?

Efficiency of Current System

39.(a) Is the committee satisfied with the present system for recruiting lay magistrates? Yes/No.

(b) Reasons for ans. (a)

40.(a) Does the committee think the present level of West Indian/Asian magistrates is satisfactory? Yes/No.

(b) If no to (a) is this because the system is inefficient? If yes to (b), please expand. If no, is there a lack of suitable candidates?)

(c) If yes to (a) is this the result of any specific action on the committee's part?

177

41. Have you anything you would like to add?

42. Is a different view taken of political activity by West Indian, etc., candidates and white candidates? Yes/No.

INTERVIEW GUIDE: CANDIDATES FOR THE BENCH WHO WITHDREW OR WERE NOT APPOINTED
(Not all questions are applicable to each category)

A. Personal

1. Name.

2. Sex.

3. Age.

4. Occupation (detail, self-employed; supervisor, etc.)

5. How long have you lived in this area?

6. Where were you born in Britain?

7. How long have you been in Britain?

8. Where is your family from originally?

9. Are you actively involved in any voluntary or community organisation? Yes/No.

10.(a) Are you a member of any political party?

   (b) How active are you? Do you hold any office within the party?

   (c) Are you a Cllr.? (What ward?) Yes/No.

11. Are you a member of any other public bodies (school governors, hospital management committees)?

B. Being Proposed for the Bench
I would like to ask about your experience of being proposed for the Bench.

12. What Bench/area were you proposed for?

13.(a) Was becoming a magistrate your idea?
   or
   (b) Did someone suggest it to you?

14. If 13(a) for what reason did you think of becoming a magistrate?

15.(a) If 13(b) why do you think you were proposed?

   (b) What was your reaction to being proposed? (reasons).

16. When were you proposed?

17.(a) Had you been proposed before? Yes/No.

   (b) How many times have you been proposed?

   (c) In this area or somewhere else?

   (d) What happened on the previous occasion(s)?

18. How did your family, friends, local community react to your (a) being proposed? (Did they approve/disapprove? Did their reaction influence whether or not the candidate continued?)

19.(a) Before becoming a magistrate, did you expect that, if appointed you would have to change your public behaviour (eg, not go on demonstrations, etc.)? Yes/No.

   (b) Did this affect your decision about whether or not to continue with your application? Yes/No.

C. Selection Procedure
Now I would like to ask you about your experience and opinion of the selection procedure.

20. Who did you have as the signatories to your application form? (J.P.s?)

21.(a) Do you know if, when you were proposed, enquiries were made about you, eg, amongst your friends? Yes/No.

   (b) If yes, what sort of information was being sought?

22.(a) How many times were you interviewed?

   (b) How long elapsed between interviews?

23.(a) How many people interviewed you (i) the first time?
       (ii) on subsequent occasions?

   (b) Were the same people on the interview panel on all occasions? Yes/No.

178

24.(a) Where did the interview(s) take place (i) the first time?
  (ii) subsequently

  (b) How long did they last (i) the first time?
  (ii) subsequently?

25. What were you asked about?

26. Were you asked whether, if appointed, you would regard yourself as a representative of the local West Indian, African and Asian population or the community as a whole? (If yes, what reply given?)

27. Were you asked about your attitude to certain types of crime? (If yes, give examples what reply given.)

28. Were you asked about your attitude towards the police? (If yes, give examples, what reply given.)

29. Were you asked about your political activity? (If yes, give examples, what reply given.)

30. What was your overall impression of your interview? (Rigorous, thorough, fair, or not so?)

D. For Candidates not Appt. (as yet) (31-36)
31.(a) When your name went forward did you consider you had as much chance of being selected as a white candidate? Yes/No.

  (b) Reasons.

32.(a) Did anything you experience during the selection process lead you to revise your expectations? Yes/No.

  (b) What?

  (c) Why did (b) have this effect?

33. Do you still consider you might be appointed? Yes/No.

34. What is your reaction to not being appointed (as yet)? (Probe effect on view of magistracy, institutions in general, race relations).

35. How have your family, friends, community reacted to you not being appointed (as yet)?

36.(a) Would you consider re-applying, going for another interview if requested? Yes/No.

  (b) Reasons for answer (a).

E. For Candidates who Withdrew
37. At what point in the selection process did you withdraw? (If not already ans.)

38. Reasons for withdrawal? (If not already ans.) (Political reasons or experience of selection process?)

39. How did your family, friends, community react to your decision to withdraw?

40.(a) Would you ever consider re-applying? Yes/No.

  (b) If yes, under what circumstances?

F. Ask Both Categories
41.(a) Are you happy with the present procedures for selecting magistrates? Yes/No.

  (b) Reasons for answer (a) (Probe possible changes.)

42.(a) Do you think selection procedure treats West Indian, etc. people in any way differently from white people? Yes/No.

  (b) Reasons for answer (a).

43. What sort of people get selected? (Why?)

G. Views on West Indians, etc. becoming Magistrates
44.(a) Do you think it important also for West Indians, etc. to get on to other public bodies and positions of authority? Yes/No.

  (b) Please give examples/expand.

45.(a) Do you think it is important for West Indians, Africans and Asians etc. to get on to the Bench? Yes/No.

  (b) Reasons for answer (a). (How important do you think it is for improving race relations?)

46. What personal qualities should magistrates have?

47.(a) Have you ever proposed anybody for the Bench? Yes/No.

  (b) Was he/she a West Indian/African/Asian, etc.? If not who?

  (c) Was he/she successful?

  (d) If unsuccessful, were any interviewed?

48.(a) have you ever been requested to give information about a candidate for the Bench? Yes/No.

  (b) What (in general terms) were you asked?

H. Magistrates' Justice
49. Do you think West Indian, African, Asian defendants have any particular difficulties in magistrates' courts which white people do not experience?

50.(a) Do members of the West Indian, African and Asian communities ever complain to you about the treatment in magistrates' courts? Yes/No.

(b) If yes, what are the most common sorts of complaint?

51.(a) Do the complainants ever make reference to whether or not there are West Indian, Africans or Asians on the Bench? Never/Occasionally/Frequently.

(b) If yes, what point are the complainants making?

(c) If no, does this surprise you?

52.(a) Have local West Indians, etc. magistrates been able to alleviate any of these difficulties or complaints? Yes/No.

(b) Examples/Reasons?

53. (If appropriate) Do you think the magistracy can be changed from within?

54.(a) Do you think magistrates should consider themselves as primarily representatives of their ethnic group? Yes/No.

(b) Why?

55. Is there anything you would like to add?

INTERVIEW GUIDE: WEST INDIAN, AFRICAN AND ASIAN MAGISTRATES

A. Personal
1. Name.

2. Sex.

3. Age.

4. Occupation (detail, self-employed; supervisor, etc.).

5. How long have you lived in this area?

6. Were you born in Britain?

7. How long have you been in Britain?

8. Where is your family from originally?

9. Are you actively involved in any voluntary or community organisations? Yes/No.

10.(a) Are you a member of any political party?

(b) How active are you, do you hold any office within the party?

(c) Are you a Cllr? (What ward?) Yes/No.

11. Are you a member of any other public bodies (school governors, hospital management committees)?

B. Becoming a Magistrate
I would now like to ask you some questions about your decision to become a magistrate.

12. What Bench do you sit on?

13. How long have you been on that Bench?

14.(a) Have you been a magistrate in any other area? Yes/No.

(b) If yes, could you give the dates?

(c) Why did you leave this Bench?

(d) Did your experiences as a magistrate in .... give rise to either negative or positive opinions about the Bench? Yes/No.

(e) Pleace expand.

(f) Did these experiences/opinions affect your decision to apply for the Bench in ....? Yes/No.

(g) Please explain answer to (f).

15. For what reasons did you think of becoming a magistrate?

16. Who proposed you? (Probe why.)

17. When were you proposed?
18.(a) Had you been proposed before? Yes/No.

(b) How many times have you been proposed?

(c) In this area or somewhere else?

(d) What happened on the previous occasion(s)?

19. Why do you think you were selected? (Also selected in other areas.)
20. How did your family, friends, local community react to your (a) being proposed, (b) being appointed?

(Probe did they approve/disapprove and why.)

21. Has the attitude of your family, friends, local community, to you being a magistrate changed now that you have been on the Bench for a while? Yes/No.

22. Before becoming a magistrate did you expect that, if appointed, you would have to change your public behaviour (eg, not go on demonstrations etc.)? Yes/No.

23.(a) Have you actually done so? Yes/No (please give examples).

(b) Was there are any pressure put on you by the court authorities? Yes/No.

C. Selection Procedure

Now I would like to ask you about your experience and opinion of the present selection procedure in some detail.

24.(a) Do you know if, when your were proposed, enquiries were made about you, eg, amongst your friends? Yes/No.

(b) If yes, what sort of information was being sought?

25.(a) How many times were you interviewed?

(b) How long elapsed between interviews?

26.(a) How many people interviewed you (i) the first time? (ii) on subsequent occasions?

(b) Were the same people on the interview panel on all occasions? Yes/No.

27.(a) Where did the interview(s) take place (i) the first time? (ii) subsequently?

(b) How long did they last (i) the first time? (ii) subsequently?

28. What were you asked about?

29. Were you asked whether, if appointed, you would regard yourself as a representative of the local West Indian, African and Asian population, or of the community as a whole? If yes, what reply given.

30. Were you asked about your attitude to certain types of crime? (If yes, give examples what reply given).

31. Were you asked about your attitude towards the police? (If yes, give examples what reply given).

32. Were you asked about your political activity? (If yes, give examples what reply given).

33. What was your overall impression of your interview? (Rigorous, thorough, fair, or not so?)

D. Characteristics of the Bench

I would like to ask you some questions about the composition of the magistracy in your area.

34. What personal qualities do you consider a magistrate should have?

35. Do you think magistrates should be professional/administrative decision-makers (human information-processing machines) or take decisions on a different basis, a gut reaction as to who 'is lying')?

36. What sort of background/experience should magistrates have (if not already covered)?

37. What sort of people do you think are chosen and why?

38.(a) Are you happy with the current composition of your local Bench? (Probe racial composition).

(b) Reasons for answer to (a).

39.(a) Are you happy with the present procedures for selecting magistrates? Yes/No.

(b) Reasons for answer (a) (Probe possible changes).

40.(a) Do you think the selection procedure treats West Indians, etc., people in any way differently from white people? Yes/No.

(b) Reasons for answer (a).

E. Experience on the Bench

I would like to ask you a few questions about your experience as a magistrate.

41.(a) Have you ever been chairman in court? Yes/No.

(b) Do you think your seniority entitles you to have been chairman? Yes/No.

42. Do you think West Indian, Asian defendants have any particular difficulties in magistrates' courts which white people do not experience?

43.(a) Do members of the West Indian, African and Asian communities ever complain to you about the treatment in magistrates' courts? Yes/No.

(b) If yes, what are the most common sorts of complaint?

(c) Please give examples.

44.(a) Do the complainants ever make reference to whether or not there are West Indian, Africans or Asians on the Bench? Never/Occasionally/Frequently.

(b) If yes, what point are the complainants making?

(c) If no, does this surprise you?

45.(a) Have you as a magistrate been able to ease any of these difficulties? Yes/No.

(b) If yes, please give examples.

181

(c) If no, why not?

46.(a) If yes to 45(a) did this involve you taking up any of these difficulties with the authorities (Clerk, chairman)? Yes/No.

(b) If yes to (a) with what result?

47.   (If appropriate) do you think the magistracy can be changed from within?

48.   As a magistrate do you regard yourself as a representative of your (ethnic) group or serving the community as a whole?

F. Views on West Indians, Africans and Asians Becoming Magistrates
Now I would like to ask you about your opinion of West Indians, Africans and/or Asians becoming magistrates.

49.(a) Do you think it is important for West Indians and Asians, etc. to get on to the Bench? Yes/No.

(b) Reasons for answer to (a). (Probe how important you think it is for improving race relations?).

50.(a) Do you think it is important for West Indians, etc., to get onto other public bodies and positions of authority? Yes/No.

(b) Please give examples/expand.

51.(a) Have you ever proposed anybody for the Bench? Yes/No.

(b) Was he/she a West Indian/African/Asian, etc., and if not who?

(c) Was he/she successful?

(d) If unsuccessful were any interviewed?

52.(a) Have you ever been requested to give information about a candidate for the Bench? Yes/No.

(b) What (in general terms) were you asked?

53.   Is there anything you would like to add?

INTERVIEW GUIDE: WEST INDIAN, AFRICAN AND ASIAN GROUPS

A. Information about the Group
1.   Name of Group.

2.   Name and Position of Interviewee.

3.   Catchment Area.

4.   Objectives.

5.   How does the group attempt to realise its objectives?

6.   How does the group make policy?

B. Magistrates' Courts
I would like to ask you some questions about your group's view(s) on the fairness of the treatment of members of your community received in magistrates' courts.

7.   What is your group's opinion about magistrates' attitude to policy evidence in cases where the defendant is West Indian, African or Asian?

8.   What are the reasons for your previous answer? (Ask for examples if appropriate).

9.(a) Have you received any complaints about magistrates? Yes/No.

(b) If yes, what are the most common complaints your group has received (over the last five years)?

(c) Please give examples.

10.(a) Do the complainants ever make reference to whether there are or are not West Indian, Africans, Asians on the Bench? Never, Occasionally, Frequently.

(b) If yes, what point are the complainants making (driving at)?

(c) If no, does this surprise you? (Reasons for answer).

C. Characteristics of the Bench

11.   What personal qualities does your group consider a magistrate should have?

12.   Do you think magistrates should be like professional/administrative decision-makers (human information-processing machines) or take decisions on a different sort of basis, a gut reaction as to who is lying?

13.   What sort of background, experience should magistrates have (if not covered by answer to 11)?

14.   What sort of people do you think are chosen?

15.   Why do you think they are chosen?

16.(a) Are you happy with the current composition of the Bench? (Probe racial composition). Yes/No.
    (b) Reasons for answer to (a).

17.(a) Are you happy with the current system of recruitment and selection to the Bench? Yes/No.
    (b) Reasons for answer to (a).

D. Attitudes to West Indian, African and Asians becoming Magistrates

18.(a) Do you think it important for West Indians, etc., to get into positions of authority? Yes/No.
    (b) Reasons for answer to (a).

19.(a) Do you think it important to increase the number of West Indian, etc., magistrates?
    (b) Reasons for answer to (a).

20.(a) If yes to (19) has your group put forward candidates for the Bench? Yes/No.
    (b) If no to (a), why not?
    (c) If yes to (a) with what results? (Were any interviewed? Were any appointed? Were any interviewed but not appointed?)

21.   Do any members of your group have any contacts with:
    (a) Magistrates Yes/No.
    (b) Members of the Advisory Committees? Yes/No.
    (c) If yes, what sort of contact?
    (d) Have you ever raised the issue of increasing the West Indian, African and Asian membership of the Bench with them? Yes/No.
    (e) If yes to (d), with what result?

22.   Have you ever signed a proposal form on anybody's behalf? Yes/No.

23.(a) Have you ever been asked about anybody who was a candidate? Yes/No.
    (b) If yes, what sort of information were you asked to give?

APPENDIX IV

DESCRIPTION OF AREAS VISITED DURING LOCAL STUDIES

The local studies were all carried out in urban areas. This was an inevitable consequence of the decision to select places where black people constituted a sizeable element of the local population. The areas visited are in three different parts of England and Wales. They vary in size, in character, in the proportion of the residents who are black, in the extent to which the local black population is of Afro-Caribbean or Indian or Pakistani origin and the number of black magistrates on the Bench.

By far the biggest area we shall call Metropole County. Unlike the other Advisory Committees or Sub-Committees included in the local studies, each of which is responsible for making recommendations for a single petty sessional division, the Metropole Committee makes recommendations for the Bench for several petty sessional divisions. These Benches cover a number of large and densely populated boroughs and thus the jurisdiction of the Metropole Committee extends over a vast area where over 1,875,000 people live and where some local centres are twenty to twenty-five miles apart.

Black people both from Asia and from Afro-Caribbean backgrounds make up a very significant proportion of the population in Metropole County. It is estimated that together they add up to nearly 15 per cent (1981 census). In none of the boroughs are they less than 5 per cent of the population and in two of the boroughs they are over 20 per cent. There are more people with an Asian background than with an Afro-Caribbean background in Metropole County as a whole, and Asians are a significant part of the population throughout the area, constituting over 3 per cent of the local population in all the boroughs and over 10 per cent in several of them. The majority of Asian families living in Metropole County migrated from India or East Africa, and they far exceed Asians who came from Pakistan and what is now Bangladesh. The number of people with a Pakistani background is only of any size in three boroughs, but these communities, which are between 2,500 and 5,000 (between 1.25 per cent and 1.75 per cent of the population of each borough) are relatively small in relation to the local Asian populations as a whole. Black people with an Afro-Caribbean background also live throughout the area. In some boroughs they are less than 2 per cent but in others they are over 10 per cent of the local population. The main points of departure for Afro-Caribbean families in Metropole County were Jamaica and Guyana.

For practical reasons, the decision was taken to concentrate on three of the petty sessional divisions (P.S.D.s) in Metropole County. The boundaries of these divisions do differ somewhat from the borough boundaries but in all of them there is a large black population, though its composition varies. Towards the west of Metropole County, in what we shall call Fridham P.S.D., the majority of black people originate from India, in particular from rural parts of the Punjab, and from East Africa. There is also a significant number of black Afro-Caribbeans in the area. Tranley P.S.D. has both a large Asian and Afro-Caribbean community. The third P.S.D., Darley, is very cosmopolitan and has a large Afro-Caribbean population and a considerably smaller, but still significant, number of people with an Indian or East African background. In common with many Afro-Caribbeans and Asians throughout Metropole County, many of those living in the areas covered by these three P.S.D.s work, when work can be found, in semi-skilled and unskilled jobs. For example, many of the Asian Indians living in Fridham work or have worked in unpleasant jobs in processing industries (food, plastic, rubber) or in catering, or in industrial cleaning. Amongst Fridham's Asian working population, however, there are also small businessmen providing services to the local Asian communities and a number of people who have 'professional' jobs in education and in welfare and community work.

The size of the Bench in Metropole County's petty sessional divisions varies considerably. Some P.S.D.s have over 120 magistrates, the largest Bench being over 140 strong. In contrast, two of the Benches have only between forty and fifty magistrates. The total number of magistrates throughout the county at the time we did our research was 729 and only twenty-eight (3.8 per cent) were black. This number does not reflect the total number of black people living in Metropole County. This is also true when we look at particular Benches. Fridham, which has a large Bench, has the most black magistrates both in terms of number and percentage with five Afro-Caribbean and five Asian magistrates, but this is still only a modest number considered in relation to the size of the local Asian population. There are four Afro-Caribbeans and three Asians on Tranley Bench, which does not reflect the significance of the local Afro-Caribbean population. Darley, which has a large Afro-Caribbean population and a much smaller, but still significant number of people with an Asian background, has three Afro-Caribbean magistrates. There are two Benches in Metropole County with no black magistrates at all.

The two other local studies were done in cities in the north of England. Branston and Harley are the centres of two large metropolitan districts with populations of nearly 700,000 and 500,000 respectively. Both are industrial and commercial centres, and much local employment is also provided by the public sector: education, health and transport. The present recession has hit the populations of both areas hard. Branston because it has a more diverse local economy has perhaps been better insulated from the harshest effects of the current economic climate. Harley has suffered badly because the rate at which its major industry is declining has become more severe. This change in Harley's local economy has been reflected in the composition of the Bench: directors and managers from this industry are no longer the main occupational group amongst the magistrates. Both cities have twilight areas not far from the city centre and just outside the inner-city road network.

Branston P.S.D. covers an area spreading out from the city centre but not taking in the whole metropolitan district. There are about 463,000 people living in this area of whom about 23,000 (5 per cent) are black (*Source:* 1981 census, Small Area statistics). People whose families came from India are the largest group amongst those with an Asian background. The only other sizable Asian national group are people whose families came from Pakistan. The Afro-Caribbean population is almost of equal size to that with an Indian background. Branston's black population lives largely in four inner-city wards. A large proportion of Branston's Afro-Caribbean population, of which most of the first generation came from the same island, live in those wards which are bordered by inner-city motorway approach roads. Most of those with work tend to be employed in semi-skilled and unskilled jobs and live in poor housing. The Afro-Caribbeans of this area tend to identify themselves, and to be identified, as a community. There are a significant number of people with an Asian background also living in this part of Branston, which we shall call Rye.

Branston has a large and busy Bench. At times there may be as many as fourteen courts sitting, including the juvenile court. At the time of the research, there were 225 magistrates (the establishment is 300) of whom seven were black (3.1 per cent) — two with an Asian background, four with an Afro-Caribbean background, and one with an African background. The first Afro-Caribbean and Asian magistrates were appointed in the late 1960s and early 1970s, but there was then a long gap and the five other magistrates have all been appointed in the last three years. It is interesting to note that four of the people recently appointed, either live in or are connected with, organisations in Rye.

Like the Branston Bench, Harley P.S.D. does not cover the whole Metropolitan district. Most of the more desirable residential suburbs and outlying towns fall under the jurisdiction of other Benches. The city court covers the inner city, which is characterised by old terraced housing and factories, many of which are now silent, but includes some more desirable residential areas towards the outskirts of the area. About 280,000 people live in the area Harley Bench has jurisdiction over, and of these, about 43,000 (15.3 per cent) are black (*Source:* 1981 Census, Small Area statistics). The number of Afro-Caribbeans is comparitively small and most of them come from one of the smaller Caribbean islands. There is a sizable proportion of people whose families originated in India, but people with a Pakistani background make up by far the largest element in Harley's black population. Many of the people who have come to Harley from Pakistan originate from the same rather poor rural area of the Pakistani part of Kashmir. Often they came as a result of visits from recruitment officers from firms in Harley's major industry. The main period of male immigration was the early 1960s. They tended to work in unskilled jobs doing night shifts, but in the 1960s, as they became more established, the decline of Harley's major industry became noticeable. The damage done to the employment prospects of Pakistani people by the decline has been compounded by companies which have continued to operate, seeking to increase productivity and reduce labour costs by reducing their labour force. Harley's large Pakistani community was the major reason we were interested in this city for our study.

Harley's Bench is nearly as large as Branston's; it has 223 magistrates, of whom twelve are black (5.4 per cent). There are two Afro-Caribbean magistrates, and of the ten with an Asian background, five are originally from India, and only four from Pakistan, which does not reflect the proportion of people from Pakistan in the local population.

The fourth local study was done in Thorburn, an industrial city in the west of the British Isles. Thorburn's growth and local economy had been based on its docks, and the local heavy industries for which it was an outlet. But these industries are now declining, the docks are almost deserted and a ship is a rare sight. The local economy now relies on small- to medium-sized manufacturing firms, in the public sector — including one of the largest hospitals in Europe — and also on the city being an administrative and shopping centre. About 266,000 people live in the area covered by the Thorburn Bench, of which 6,700 are black (2.5 per cent). (*Source:* 1981 Census, Small Area statistics). However, as elements of Thorburn's black population, including those of an Afro-Caribbean background, were established before the First World War, the number of black Britons in Thorburn is likely to be considerably higher than can be identified from the census statistics. As well as having a significant number of people whose families originally came from the Caribbean, Thorburn also has a significant number of people with an Asian background, of which the largest group came from India.

We were told that sometimes there could be as many as ten courts in session in Thorburn P.S.D.. At the time of the research, there were 171 magistrates on Thorburn Bench, and only three (1.75 per cent) could be described as black. Two of these were the only black magistrates we met who had been born in Britain. Of Thorburn's three black magistrates, one had been on the Bench for about fourteen years, but the other two had only been magistrates for two years.

The fifth local study was done in Meadowport, also in the west of Britain. Like Thorburn, Meadowport's initial wealth was built on its docks, which are also now largely deserted. But it is perhaps an indicator of the relative economic fortunes of the two cities that, whereas Thorburn's dockland is largely derelict, the first phase of the redevelopment plans for Meadowport's docks is already complete, and further plans are in hand.

Meadowport's Bench covers an area in which about 308,000 people live, of whom about 11,300 are black (3.7 per cent) (*Source:* 1981 Census, Small Area statistics). Afro-Caribbeans are the majority of Meadowport's black population. Most of Meadowport's Afro-Caribbean population has its origins in the migration beginning in the 1950s. The beginning of the present Afro-Caribbean population in Meadowport was a little earlier, when a number of Afro-Caribbeans who had been in the RAF settled there after being demobbed in 1945. The majority of arrivals in Meadowport from the Caribbean came from Jamaica, with Barbados being the other main point of departure. Meadowport's Jamaicans tend to work in unskilled and semi-skilled jobs and live in the city's poorer housing. There is also a sizable number of people with an Asian background, of whom the majority originate from India.

187

Meadowport's P.S.D. can be as busy as the other areas we visited, with sometimes seven, not including juvenile, courts in session. There is a large Bench of 239 magistrates, of whom six are black (2.5 per cent): four Afro-Caribbeans, one African and one Asian. Two of the Afro-Caribbean magistrates have been on the Bench for more than ten years, the most senior one for over sixteen years. But three of the other black magistrates have only two years seniority.

APPENDIX V

NOTES AND FORMS FROM LORD CHANCELLOR'S DEPT. AND A.C.s RELATING TO THE SELECTION OF CANDIDATES

Secretary of Commissions Office
Neville House
Page Street
IN CONFIDENCE London SW1P 4LS

CANDIDATES FOR THE MAGISTRACY
NOTES ON INTERVIEW PROCEDURE

1. This is a constantly developing subject and much has been learned about it in various parts of the country in the past year or two. Conditions vary from place to place and it is not practical to devise a procedure which would be acceptable everywhere. Several Advisory Committees have, however, produced very good interview instructions and the aim of these Notes is to make a selection from their ideas available to others.

2. There are many points about interviewing candidates which Advisory Committees have to resolve, for example:

(a) When should an interview be carried out? For what proportion of the candidates? And how are those to be interviewed selected for this purpose from the list?

(b) Who should carry out the interview task?

(c) Where is it best done?

(d) What procedure should be followed?

(e) What is the role of the secretary and/or Clerk to the Justices?

(f) Should the Committee as a whole take the results of interviews into account when deciding which candidates to recommend for appointment?

3. There are a number of alternatives, and discussion on their advantages, in the light of local conditions, can be undertaken by the Lord Chancellor's representative when he is invited to any Advisory Committee or Sub-Committee meeting. From these meetings good ideas developed locally may be passed on to others, without revealing the source. If any Committee has a good procedure, *pro-forma* or other aid to interviewing, which they are willing to make available to others, the Lord Chancellor would be grateful to receive a copy. Meanwhile there are attached three

189

documents, which you may find useful. They are based on current practice in a number of areas.

Document A
4. The interview form marked 'A' contains some sensible ideas for questioning and assessing. One particular Committee always starts by checking through the answers already on the candidate's Recommendation Form before embarking on the interview form itself. This serves three purposes:
(a) It puts the candidate at ease by asking him questions about himself which he has no difficulty in answering.
(b) It ensures that the information on the Recommendation Form is accurate.
(c) It establishes whether an absolute or limited disqualification may exist (e.g., has he close relatives in the local Police Force which would disqualify him?).

During this process the candidate is also asked for fuller details about his employment and about any convictions or court orders. As regards convictions, record when, where, what for and what sentence, and ask whether any cases are pending.

Document B
5. The second document attached, marked 'B', is entitled 'Suggestions for interviewing prospective candidates'. One Committee forms its interview panels (as the paper indicates) with a member of the A.C. plus two magistrates. There are several arguments for and against this composition, which it is not necessary to spell out here, and many Committees prefer to keep the choice of interviewers limited to A.C. or S.C. members; but, in any case, not less than two people should be included in the panel and three is the ideal number.

6. Particular attention should be drawn to paragraph two, especially the last sentence 'A note will be kept . . .' This might be thought to go without saying, but this practice is not always followed.

7. Motivation is a most important consideration. The candidate must not only be willing to become a magistrate but have the right reasons. A desire for social status, for example, is not acceptable. On the reverse of Document 'B' are some forms of question to explore the motivation of candidates and the extent to which they have taken the trouble to discover anything about the work. A selection from them might usefully be made by those entrusted with the interview task.

Probing the Background
8. Paragraph 27 of the Directions for Advisory Committees, says:

27. The Lord Chancellor cannot emphasise too often or too emphatically that the first and much the most important consideration in the selection and appointment of justices is that the candidates should be personally suitable in point of character, integrity and understanding and should be generally recognised as such by those among whom they live and

work. He assumes, as indeed he must assume, that only persons who are so qualified are recommended to him by an Advisory Committee and he will not, in any circumstances, approve the appointment of individuals in regard to whom these desiderata are not fully satisfied. It follows from this that a special responsibility rests with every member of a Committee and Sub-Committee who proposes a candidate for appointment to satisfy himself or herself as to the character, qualities, capacity and antecedents of a candidate. When persons known to have strong political, religious or other opinions are under consideration they should be carefully scrutinised for the presence or absence of a judicial mind, which may be defined as the capacity to be aware that their personal views may be a potential danger to their impartiality and the willingness and ability to overcome this danger. Committees and Sub-Committees should also take into account the impression which any candidate's presence on the Bench may make upon the public.

9. There is, thus, a considerable responsibility carried by the interview panel, whose report will have great influence on the Advisory Committee's eventual recommendations to the Lord Chancellor. The panel must really probe if they are to satisfy themselves 'as to the character, qualities, capacity and antecedents of a candidate' and the impression which that candidate's presence on the Bench may make upon the public. *The interview should therefore seek to discover if anything at all in the candidate's personal, business or family affairs (either past or pending) which, if it became public knowledge, might bring embarrassment or adverse publicity to the candidate, his colleagues on the same Bench or to the magistracy as a whole.*

10. Problems arise, from time to time, with serving magistrates who incur convictions, or whose spouses or children incur them, or who are involved in some sort of proceedings not necessarily leading to a conviction but potentially damaging to public confidence in the probity and impartiality of the magistracy. The decision on what action is necessary rests with the Lord Chancellor. It could be that the magistrate is rebuked and reminded of the need to be more careful in observing the law. In more serious cases he might be suspended from sitting for a time. In still more serious cases he might be invited to consider the propriety of resigning. He might even be removed from the Commission.

11. Clearly it would be highly illogical for a candidate to be recommended for appointment when any of these forms of action might be necessary. That is why it is important to ensure, as far as possible, by suitable questioning at interview that there is nothing of this nature in his background. If rejection or deferment is not the answer, the facts disclosed must be clearly brought to the notice of the Advisory Committee and ultimately the Lord Chancellor for his decision.

12. This probing and the final comprehensive question underlined in paragraph nine, seem to be the most important part of the whole thing. Nearly all the selection misfortunes of the recent past would have been avoided, or at least much more easily dealt with, if this question had been asked with the proper build-up and context.

Document C

13. The third document attached, marked 'C', is another county's interview form. The front side of this is largely a repeat of the old Recommendation Form: but para.19 on the reverse side provides a very good assessment form (simpler than the one at 'A' and therefore preferred by some Committees). Moreover, the 'key' final question is set out in full at para.19(h).

14. A useful comment to make to the candidate before putting this question to him is: 'As you know, if you become a magistrate you could become a target for criticism, in the local papers for example. There will be no lack of people only too ready to criticise your appointment and your subsequent actions; anything that can be dredged up about you will be regarded in some quarters as fair comment and a matter of public interest. So, is there anything at all . . . etc.? The interviewer can then add, if he wishes: 'You need not reveal the precise details at this interview if you prefer not to. But, if there is anything of that nature and on reflection you wish to withdraw from being considered for appointment, or you feel we should know about it, now is the time to say so.'

General Points

15. Some Committees have said in the past that they had held back from interviewing or delegated the task in a way which really did not meet the Lord Chancellor's wish that no candidate should be recommended for appointment unless known or interviewed by a member of an Advisory Committee or Sub-Committee. This was because they were worried about a possible loss of anonymity.

16. To meet this, most of the interview panels preface their enquiries with some statement by the Chairman on these lines:

> I shall not introduce myself and my colleagues to you by name. *We are a group of local magistrates** who have been asked to interview you. We shall ask you some very searching personal questions and expect you to give absolutely straightforward answers. This interview is strictly confidential and I promise you that nothing you reveal here will be allowed to leak to outsiders. In the same way, we rely upon you to treat the whole interview as confidential and not to reveal anything about it to anyone else, not even the identity of any of us whom you may recognise.

17. Chairmen frequently end the interview by again reminding candidates of the confidentiality of the proceedings, emphasising that the ability to be totally discreet in confidential matters is an essential characteristic in a magistrate.

18. At some stage, and preferably at the end, candidates should be told that there are always many more applicants than vacancies; not everyone invited for interview will be appointed, and not to be appointed does not in

---

*If one (or more) of the interview panel is not a magistrate, this may be revised to 'We are a group, including some local magistrates, who have . . .'

192

any way imply inferiority or unsuitability. It is necessary to take into account many other factors to ensure a good balance of representation on the Bench. For instance there must be a spread of ages, of both sexes, of socio-economic and employment backgrounds and even of political persuasions, in addition to geographical coverage, if the Bench is to be representative of a true cross-section of the community. The chairman may like to say: 'The final choice does not lie with the Interview Panel, of course, nor even with the Advisory Committee; it rests entirely with the Lord Chancellor personally and he may, or may not, accept the recommendations of his Advisory Committee.'

T.C. Spicer
Assistant Secretary of Commissions   *January 1980*

CONFIDENTIAL

LORD CHANCELLOR'S ADVISORY COMMITTEE   'A'
INTERVIEWS

RECOMMENDED
NOT RECOMMENDED

Name of Candidate   Date of Interview

Residence: Is applicant settled in area or likely to move?

Family Background:
Any close relative on Bench: No/Yes

In local Police: No/Yes

Practising law locally: No/Yes

Positions held since leaving school: Period. Comments.

Hobbies and Special Interests
Voluntary Organisations

Religion/Church Work

Sport

Spare-time Interests

Candidate's Health: Any serious illness or disability.

Is applicant under consideration for appointment to any other Commission of the Peace Area? Yes/No.

Define Work and Training Involved
Is Candidate interested in serving on Juvenile Panel? Domestic Panel?

Has Candidate ever visited a Magistrates' Court? A Crown Court?

Time to do this work. To undertake the full training.

ASSESSMENT FORM
Immediate impression of Candidate? A, B, C, D, E

Manner: Shy, nervous, quiet, cheerful, relaxed, impassive, dull.

Speech: Over-refined, satisfactory, average, indistinct, too broad to be intelligible.

Ability to express views: Fluent, clear, forceful, satisfactory, uncertain, poor.

Temperament: Balanced and mature, average, lacking depth, very superficial.

Desirable Qualities:						Undesirable Qualities:
Reasonable	A	B	C	D	E	Irrational
Alert and interested	A	B	C	D	E	Uninterested, slow to respond
Intelligent	A	B	C	D	E	Dull

Patient, a good listener	A B C D E	Impatient, tends to interrupt
Able to put opinions	A B C D E	Lacking ideas or the ability to express them
Flexible views	A B C D E	Dogmatic views
Ability to see other's viewpoint	A B C D E	Self-centred, unsympathetic
Ability to make judgements	A B C D E	Uncertain, vacillating
Impartial and objective	A B C D E	Prejudiced or intolerant

General Impression:

| *Outstanding* | *Possible but Very Good* | *Not suitable Suitable* | *Doubtful* | *In my view* |
| A | B | C | D | E |

| | | *Average* | | |

Committee's assessment:

QUESTIONS TO CANDIDATES

1. Alternative Questions to Explore Motivation

(a) *You must have a picture of what is involved in being a magistrate. Where did you get it? Whom did you ask?*

(b) *Why would you like to be a magistrate?*

(c) *What do you think is the main part of a magistrate's work?*

(d) *Have you any misgivings about judging people, convicting them, imposing penalties upon them?*

(e) *Is your motivation primarily to help people who are in trouble with the law, i.e. welfare opportunity?*

(f) *What is your picture of what is involved in the work?*

(g) *How long have you been interested in this sort of work?*

(h) *Have you ever visited a magistrates' court or any other court, perhaps a Crown Court? Why not, if you are interested in being a magistrate?*

(i) *If you have never been in court, on what do you base your feelings that you would be interested in the work or have something to offer to it?*

(j) *Do you think you would be good at this work?*

(k) *Do you have any views on sentencing and how various offences should be dealt with?*

(l) *Do you think the police ought to be supported as far as possible?*

(m) *What is it that aroused your interest in the magistracy?*

1A. Supplementary Questions Asked to a Pakistani Immigrant Candidate

(a) *Would you regard yourself, if you became a magistrate, as in some way representing the Pakistani community?*

(b) *Do you think that, if you became a magistrate, members of the Pakistani community would regard you as in some respect representing them on the Bench? Would their attitude towards you put you under any pressure and how would you cope with it?*

ADVISORY COMMITTEE 'B'
SUGGESTIONS FOR INTERVIEWING PROSPECTIVE CANDIDATES

1. Arrangement:-
A member of the Advisory Committee together with two magistrates meets each prospective candidate for half an hour to discuss aspects of the work of a Justice of the Peace and the interests and ideas of the candidate. This meeting should not have the atmosphere of a formal interview; consider sitting the candidate between the interviewers rather than have him facing an interviewing court.

2. Chairman:-
The chairman can begin by 'going through' the original recommendation with the candidate. He will steer the discussion to seek out for example any stray prejudices, emotional or intellectual reactions by the candidate, and on the other hand the qualities of a good magistrate: patience, knowledge of people, ready grasp of situations, ability to listen, sound judgement etc.. A note will be kept, and after the meeting it will be decided what advice should go to the Advisory Committee.

3. Magistrates
One of the magistrates can then be asked to comment on aspects of the work of a Justice. These comments could include:

(a) *Court Attendances* — at least twenty-six half days a year (actual average in . . . is about thirty-five) and usually confined to a morning or afternoon although magistrates are generally expected to be available for the whole of their court day.

(b) *Kind of work* — hearing criminal cases (over 98 per cent of the total), dealing with traffic offenders, hearing domestic cases (husband and wife, children), juvenile-court work (children in need of care and protection as well as delinquents), licensing work (public houses, clubs, entertainment licences, gaming, betting, probation and police committees, Crown Court attendances.

(c) *Training* — detailed initial training (partly at the University), later advanced training in chairmanship, sentencing exercises and conferences, meetings with various organisations to discuss various problems. Both giving and receiving talks, taking part in debates, etc., if that happens to be of interest. Visits to penal and other institutions.

(d) *Applications* of various sorts which are made to a Justice. From signing papers (e.g. passport applications) to hearing applications for warrants to search premises or for the hearing of summonses. Some may be at own home or business.

4. The Candidate:-
Should be given plenty of opportunity to express opinions and to ask questions. The candidate's views on some of the following may be interesting:-

How effective are our present means of keeping law and order and dealing with crime (views on imprisonment etc.)?

Has he heard much about the drugs problem?

How does he feel about the way the law affects the motorist (fixed penalities, driving and drinking, speed in fog)?

Reactions to press reports of cases?

Cause and cure of football hooliganism?

What does he think of English licensing laws (any continental experience?), and about the social pastimes of bingo, betting, gaming?

Importance of marriage and the family in modern society (link with juvenile delinquency)?

Views on the prevalence of shop-lifting?

How important is people's appearance?

LORD CHANCELLOR'S ADVISORY COMMITTEE FOR   'C'
Advisory Sub-Committee....
Appointment to Commission of the Peace
Report on Interview by ....

1. Name of candidate:

2. Address: Tel No.

3. Date of Birth:

4. Single/Married/Widowed/Divorced.

5. Age(s) and sex(es) of children:

6. Academic, professional or trade qualifications:

7. Occupation:
       Status in employment, and
       Jobs undertaken:

8. Husband's or Wife's occupation:

9. Is the candidate related to an existing Justice?

10. Previous employment:

11. Social Work: (a) Dates:

                                     (b) Position in it:

12. Other outside interests:

    Involvement   Time Spent:

13. Political views:

14. (a) Health: (b) Hearing: (c) Sight:

15. Criminal Offences (if any — including motoring offences):

16. Name, address and occupation of the person(s) recommending the Candidate:

17. Date of Recommendation:

18. Time to carry out duties

19. Interviewer's assessment of candidate:
   (a) Intelligence:

(b) Fair-mindedness:

(c) Any hobby-horses:

(d) Presence:

(e) Speech delivery:

(f) Ability to make decisions:

(g) Ability to listen without interrupting:

(h) Any question marks, if so, on what grounds:

Is there anything at all in your personal business or family affairs (either past or pending) which if it became public knowledge might bring embarrassment or adverse publicity to you, to your colleagues on the same Bench, or to the magistracy as a whole?

(i) Recommendation:

Signed .... Date...

Note:

1. Questions 1-16 have been included from the information on the candidates' recommendation forms and should be updated at the interview.

2. The candidates should be told that there are always more applicants than there are vacancies and that the final decision rests with the Lord Chancellor. Also that they will not hear any more of the application, or the result of the interview, unless they receive a formal offer of appointment from the Lord Chancellor's Office.

Recommendations for Interviewing Candidates by one Advisory Committee to its sub-Committees

INTERVIEW PROCEDURE

1. Prior to each interview the Clerk to the Justices will see each candidate to verify the accuracy of the information on the nomination form.

2. The Chairman will welcome each candidate and will make the following statement to each of them:

I shall not introduce myself and my colleagues to you by name. We are a group of local magistrates who have been asked to interview you. We shall ask you some very searching personal questions and expect you to give absolutely straightforward answers. This interview is strictly confidential and I assure you that nothing that you say in here will be passed to anybody outside. In the same way, we rely upon you to treat the interview as confidential and not to reveal anything about it to anyone else, not even the identity of any one of us whom you may recognise.

3. The Chairman will then ask each candidate to answer two or three factual questions from the nomination form, in order to put him at his ease, and will then ask the following questions:-

(a) Why would you like to be a magistrate and why do you think you would make a good magistrate?

(b) Have you any misgivings about judging people, convicting them, and imposing penalities upon them?

(c) Have you ever visited a magistrates' court or any other court?

(d) Do you have any views on sentencing and how various offences should be dealt with?

(e) How do you feel about the way the law affects the motorist?

(f) Would you comment on the cause and possible cure of football hooliganism?

(g) The Lord Chancellor's requirements in respect of attendances at court are very stringent. Can you assure us that you have the time and the will to carry out these duties?

(h) Give further details of any convictions or court orders on the nomination form, or if none, confirm that there are none either past or pending.

(i) Is there anything at all in your personal, business or family affairs, either past or pending, which if it became public knowledge might bring embarrassment or adverse publicity, or both, to you, to your colleagues on the same Bench or to the magistracy as a whole?

4. The Chairman will ask if any member of the panel would like to ask a follow-up question or questions to the candidates and he will also give an opportunity to each candidate to ask questions of the panel.

5. The chairman will conclude each interview by saying:-

I would like to remind you, as I said at the start of the interview, that what has been said here today is strictly confidential on both sides.

An essential characteristic of a magistrate is that he or she should be totally discreet in confidential matters and you can imagine the damage which could be done by any magistrate who was unreliable in this respect.

The Lord Chancellor, on whose behalf we are interviewing you, has also asked me to tell you that as there are always more applicants than vacancies not everyone invited for interview will be appointed. Not to be appointed does not in any way imply inferiority or unsuitability since it is necessary to take into account many other factors to ensure a good balance of representation on the Bench. For instance there must be a spread of ages, of both sexes, of socio-economic and employment backgrounds and even of political persuasions, in addition to geographical coverage, if the Bench is to be truly representative of the community.

When we have completed the interviews our recommendations will be sent to the Lord Chancellor's Advisory Committee who in turn will send their recommendations to the Lord Chancellor. It rests entirely with him personally to appoint magistrates and he may, or may not, accept the recommendations of his Advisory Committee.

IN CONFIDENCE

PARTICULARS OF A PERSON TO BE CONSIDERED FOR APPOINTMENT AS A JUSTICE OF THE PEACE

1. Name of candidate (in full)
   (state maiden name, decorations or honours where applicable)

2. Address

   Post Code   Tel. No.

3. For how long has the candidate lived in the district?

4. Place of birth

5. Nationality   6. Single/married/widowed/divorced/separated

7. Sexes and ages of children (if any)

8. Academic, professional or trade qualifications

9. (a) Occupation or position held

   (b) Name and address of employer

   (c) Place of employment   Tel. No.

10. Any previous employment

11. Husband's or wife's occupation

12. (a) Social work at present time

    (b) Any experience relevant to the duties of a magistrate

    (c) Other interests

13. Is the candidate related to an existing Justice?

    If yes, state relationship and the Justice's Bench

14. (a) Is the candidate, or has he been, a police officer, special constable or traffic warden? (If so, please give particulars, with dates, of service and Force of which a member or of the area(s) of warden's duties).

    (b) Is the candidate related to:
        (i) a police officer, special constable or traffic warden? (If so, please give particulars of (1) relationship and (2) Force or the area(s) of warden's duties.)

        (ii) any person having business before the courts for the County/area, such as a court official, solicitor, or probation or welfare officer? (If so, please give particulars)

15. Is the candidate a member of a local authority (other than a parish council)?

16. Political views of the candidate (how does he normally vote?)
    [The candidate's political views are neither a qualification nor a disqualification for appointment. This information is required only in order to avoid the appointment of a disproportionate number of Justices supporting any one party]

17. Has the candidate (a) good health

                (b) good hearing without/with hearing aid

                (c) good sight (with glasses if worn)?

18. Does the candidate hold a full driving licence?

19. Has the candidate ever been convicted of a criminal offence, *including motoring offences*, or been the subject of any order, civil or criminal, made by a court of law? (If so, please give particulars including the name of the court, the date of disposal, the offence or the nature of the civil proceeding, and the penalty or order.)
N.B. The Secretary of State has by order excluded candidates for the office of Justice of the Peace from the protection of subsections (2) and (3) of section 4 of the Rehabilitation of Offenders Act 1974 for the purposes of this paragraph, and all previous convictions, however minor, must accordingly be disclosed.

20. Is the candidate defendant in any pending court proceedings?

21. Can the candidate, if appointed, carry out a fair share of magisterial duties?

22. (a) Has the candidate previously been appointed to, or proposed for, any other Commission of the Peace? If so, which and when?

    (b) Is the candidate at present under consideration for appointment to any other Commission of the Peace? If so, which?

       Candidate

       The above information is correct. My date of birth is   /   /

              My age is   ☐

       Signature   Date

23. *Person(s) recommending* the above candidate. We/I recommend this candidate for the

       Bench

   (1) Name   Address

      Occupation

      I have known the candidate for   years

      Signature   Date

   (2) Name   Address

      Occupation

      I have known the candidate for   years

      Signature   Date